BRACE for IMPACT

Heritage Associates

ALSO BY THOMAS A. LEWIS

The Shenandoah in Flames

The Guns of Cedar Creek

For King and Country

The Wildlife of North America

West from Shenandoah

BRACE for IMPACT

Surviving the Crash
of the Industrial Age

Thomas A. Lewis

SECOND EDITION

For Kathleen
in whose presence it is impossible
to be a pessimist.

CONTENTS

Introduction

The Ultimate Trap

It is one of the most compelling videos I never saw. It was described to me, as I recall, as a commercial of some kind that aired years ago in Canada. The scene is a crowded escalator in some busy store or subway station that without warning clanks to a stop. For a few moments the crowd simply stands there, staring straight ahead, waiting for the escalator to start moving again. Then they begin looking around and at each other with rising anxiety, until a few of them at first, then virtually all of them, begin calling loudly for help.

There simply is no better way to visualize what is happening to us in this new American century. We are trapped on an escalator. We have forgotten how to walk. We have accepted as our due the blandishments of industrial technology. With an élan that would make Marie Antoinette blush, we diddle the switches around us to make sure our air temperature stays at 68 degrees, humidified or dehumidified depending on the season, the texture of our ice cream is just right, our bath is steamy and our instant dinner micro-waved just so. And we give not a thought to what we have lost.

In this we are like the Native Americans who five hundred years ago joyously accepted from white men the gifts of iron pots, steel knives and firearms. They were not gifts, or course, they were token payments for the furs that were making the white men rich. A generation or so later, when the fur-bearing animals were all dead and the gifts were withdrawn, the People did not remember how to hunt, grow, prepare or cook their food. Helpless in a land of plenty, they were herded onto reservations to live out their lives on welfare.

The gifts of our technology are not gifts, either. They have made a lot of people rich. And those people have used their wealth not only to live well -- after all, we all do -- but to distract us from the fact that our counterparts to the fur-bearing animals of old, our oil and potable water and topsoil and agreeable climate are nearly all gone, and our gifts are about to be withdrawn. They don't arrest us native Americans and make us live on reservations any more, it's a lot easier to give us television to watch, filled with comedies and murder mysteries and reassuring messages about how the largest corporations are creating jobs for us and making sure the planet is going to be OK.

When the TV screen flickers off and the microwave won't wave any more, are we going to sit helplessly in our leather recliners and cry for help? When the super-grocery-mart is empty because the trucks and planes can't move the mangoes from Asia and the lettuce from California any more, are we going to wander the barren aisles, yelling for help? Will we remember anything we all once knew about hunting, growing, preparing or cooking food? Or will we be marooned on an escalator, waiting for rescue?

End of Story

It is our great misfortune to be living at the end of an age. It would be great fun, although a little dangerous, to be in on the beginning of an era. Think what it would have been like to be there when this one started, when everyone was an inventor, an explorer, a thinker of new things. Perhaps the greatest sustained pleasure is to be had in the middle decades -- think the 1950s – when your people bestride the world like a Colossus, Mother Nature herself bends to your will and life is draped with ease, luxury and the promise of more. Then, always, the end comes. It's coming now. You know it.

We are as people on an airliner flying through the night, hearing odd noises from the engines, a strange rushing wind over the fuselage, a slightly inappropriate tilt to the cabin, but we have been reluctant to take our eyes from the movie screen, or relinquish our hold on our drink, to find out what is happening, because whatever we find out probably won't be good. At some level, we know, and we have known for a while now. But as long as we don't know for sure, we can keep the dread contained, down in the basement of our mind. If we go forward into the cockpit, and there's nobody there, what then? If we look out the window and see the ground coming up at us, what's the point in that?

It's time. Time to go forward, to look out the window. Time to brace for impact.

Every system in the web of life on which our survival depends, and every human institution devised to maintain our welfare, is breaking down. Implacably increasing stresses of our own making on all these systems and institutions have made it inevitable that in the near future, one or more of them will fail, setting off a catastrophic cascade of effects.

The notion of impending cataclysm runs counter to the chamber-of-commerce optimism that is pervasive in our political and commercial speech. It is not mentioned on the Sunday talk shows or in campaign speeches. It is not well tolerated as cocktail-party chatter. ("Is this," asked a charming hostess not long ago as I warmed to this subject, "the point where I smile brightly, and edge away?") A sunny faith in the ability of technology to solve any problems that confront us is universally preferred. Nevertheless, as we will see, technology is not the solution, it is the problem.

The case made here is different from the new orthodoxy that has formed (among all but Republican candidates for president) around the issue of global warming. I have no doubt that climate change is real, man-made, and that its effects, will be disastrous. Yet they are probably going to be more subtle and remote than many of the other dangers we face. I do not mean by this to play down the dangers posed by climate change, but rather to raise the profile of the other threats we face.

Whatever chance we had to avert climate change passed decades ago. There is now no chance -- make no mistake, the probability is zero -- that we will find the political will to do the difficult things required to reduce drastically and soon our emissions of the greenhouse gases that are trapping heat in our atmosphere. If we did manage to take some moderately difficult steps in the right direction, the probability that they would significantly change the course of global warming is vanishingly small. The damage has already been done, and the resulting processes will run until a new planetary equilibrium is achieved. It may well take a thousand years.

Meanwhile, the chances are very good that some other crisis -- affecting our supply of food, for example, or of water or energy -- will threaten our survival long before the worst effects of global warming are felt.

Whatever you prefer to call this age that is ending -- the Industrial Revolution, the American Century, the Global Economy, or something else -- its origins lie three hundred years or so in the past, when those who thought of themselves as civilized people came to believe that the world they inhabited was a machine, and that they could run it.

A metaphor can be a powerful assistant, organizer, even director of thought and communication. Imagine how you would explain the ocean to a person who had never seen it. It is like a swimming pool, you might say, only bigger. The water is like the water in your tap, only saltier. The waves are like the ripples on Grandpa's pond, but huge, slow-moving and noisy. Metaphors, like words themselves, do not contain or convey meaning; they hint at meaning. Each metaphor contributes a piece of an attribute allowing the listener, you can only hope, to assemble something like the concept of ocean that you are trying to get across.

It is always a mistake to substitute the metaphor for the reality. The ocean is not a big bathtub. If a man tells his wife that she is like a beautiful movie star, he will be richly blessed for the compliment. She will understand his meaning: that in certain respects -- her pouty lips, perhaps, or flashing eyes -- she reminds him of Angelina Jolie. If, however, he comes to believe that she _is_ Angelina Jolie, he is likely to face an involuntary commitment to treatment. Yet we -- the whole modern world -- are quite comfortable in the mistaken belief that the world does not just resemble a machine, it _is_ one.

It may be useful, for example, to say the human body is like a machine in the way it uses food as fuel, converting it to energy to perform work. But the comparison merely hints at the incomprehensible complexity of what "fuels" the body can use, what processes convert them to energy and what further processes use that energy in work. Anyone who limits their understanding of the body to that one metaphor is in danger of doing serious harm.

Yet the metaphor of body-as-machine is vastly useful to the purveyors of, for example, drugs and industrialized foodstuff. You cannot watch television for an hour without seeing some simplistic animation explaining how a medication works, or a claim that something you ingest will have a predictable, straightforward and uniform effect. The success of these relentless voices is such that they have turned an astounding proportion of us into obese, over-medicated blobs looking for a magic pill to fix our "machines."

Similarly, it is one thing to observe that in certain limited respects, some processes in the world have a machine-like rigidity of cause and effect; it is quite another to believe the entire world operates as a machine and can be managed as such. The belief is held and insistently promulgated by those in line to make fortunes from selling us chemicals and implements with which to fix the various perceived deficiencies in the machine. As with our bodies, the effects of treating the whole planet as if it really were a machine -- instead of the wondrously complex, living organism that it is -- are similar, but worse by several orders of magnitude.

Now, the era made by the people who believed that the world is a machine, and that they could run it better, is staggering to its end under the accumulated weight of all the mistakes that arose from those two assumptions.

Running on Empty

We are running out of food. Never mind the commercials for Archer Daniels Midland, or the speeches of the farm-belt politicians, about the productivity of the American farmer. The American farmer -- who today is typically a suited CEO, not the overalls-clad yeoman of Grant Wood's painting *American Gothic* -- has squandered his inheritance of topsoil, fouled our air and water, denuded the ecosystem of essential species, become an incurable petroleum addict, and created a system of monoculture that invites disaster as a dry forest invites fire.

We are running out of water. Our governors have not made, or allowed anyone else to make, any calculations of the actual effects of our mindless urban sprawl or our mindless agricultural practices. (How else would you describe making a desert -- the Imperial Valley of California -- the nation's principal source of lettuce, one of the thirstiest plants known, using government-subsidized water piped in from 80 miles away?) Our aquifers are dropping, our reservoirs are shrinking, and the day comes ever closer when a large metropolitan area suddenly will have nothing to drink. (In the late fall of 2007, metro Atlanta's five million souls were declared to be 90 days away from exactly that.) Yet no government agency has the guts to require, nor any other group the good sense to try, conservation of water in any substantial way.

We are running out of oil. There is a finite amount of it, and the demand curve is climbing like a jet fighter trying to escape a heat-seeking missile. Predictions about when we will run out are usually comfortably in the future, but the real trouble -- the end game, in fact -- begins on the day the world realizes that a condition known as peak oil has been reached. All oil production follows the same pattern, as Shell Oil geologist M. King Hubbert explained in 1958: after discovery, a rapid increase, then a kind of plateau leading to peak production, then an ever-increasing falloff to nothing. That is true of individual wells, and also true of all the wells in the world taken together. United States production peaked in 1970 and has been falling, ever more steeply, since. World production is either at, approaching, or slightly past peak depending on whose calculation you credit. The point is that very soon after peak oil production is reached, there will come a day when an order for oil cannot be filled *at any price*. That is the day that all hell breaks loose.

We are running out of money. Our government, and our people are living on credit, spending more than they take in, saving nothing, and ignoring the accumulating debt that already is large enough to smother the next generations. Large corporations are doing well, despite the recent meltdown of the Casino Economy, by importing cheap goods or expensive oil, while selling little overseas except dubious financial instruments, with the result that massive amounts of our currency have accumulated in the hands of other countries.

We are running out of time.

Meanwhile our government, whose foremost responsibility is to protect us from harm, does nothing, plans nothing, and says nothing about the prospects for catastrophe. Before Hurricane Katrina, few believed such a statement; now, few can doubt it. With rare exceptions (for compelling reason, which we will discuss in Chapter Five), no politicians will discuss the gravity of the multiple threats that face us. Our media step gingerly here, balancing every news account of impending crisis with an opposing view from some technology guru. Suggestions that everything could break down are relegated to action movies and tabloid-like documentaries on cable channels (*When Yellowstone Erupts* was a recent example).

Who, Me?

And who am I to be predicting the collapse of society? How many collapses have I witnessed, personally? What degrees in catastrophe do I possess?

This book is a review of readily available information, across many disciplines and fields of endeavor, from which it draws logical conclusions. It is the work of a generalist, not a specialist. We are trained by our industrial society to subdue common sense and listen only to the advice of experts, high priests of technology who tell us what to grow and eat, how to use chemicals to make everything better, what the latest gifts of technology might be. We have forgotten the value of generalists who gaze across the rutted tracks of the specialties and notice that where we want to go is not in that direction.

In the late 1960s, the science of geology was transformed by a massive paradigm shift -- the sudden acceptance of plate tectonics. One of the experts confounded by this change described it this way: we were busily examining the planks in the deck, he said, when someone looked up and noticed that the ship was moving. That someone was a generalist.

I am an expert on experts. I have been interviewing them all my professional life, and then trying to translate what they said into comprehensible English. I have identified a syndrome -- I call it "creeping expertise" -- that affects people who come to know more and more about less and less. The more an expert knows about a thing, the less interested he is in the things everybody else knows about that thing. Pretty soon even the stuff other experts know become old hat, and a guy who once could talk engagingly about the Civil War Battle of Gettysburg is now consumed by the role of the commander of the 52nd Ohio Regiment on the late afternoon of the second day. The only way he can talk to an ordinary mortal is to get a translator or go through a de-expertification program. I'm the translator, and I'm a generalist. I have talked to the experts from biologist to volcanologist, have translated their arcane speech into English, and have merged one with another.

Allow me a personal word about how I came to this position. From 1960, when I was 18 years old, to 2003, while making my living as a journalist, I was continually involved in political and environmental activism. I served at the management level in political campaigns for offices ranging from small-town council to President of the United States (in Howard Baker's 1980 run I was, albeit briefly because of his withdrawal from the race, responsible for three states). During this time among other things I was the principal editor of the Time-Life Books series on the earth sciences, "Planet Earth," and for six years wrote the authoritative "EQ Index," an annual review of the state of the environment in the United States, for *National Wildlife* Magazine and the *World Almanac*. I am the author of five other books, four on American history and one on American wildlife.

I have been alarmed about the trends described herein for more than 25 years. During the 1980s and 1990s, I did not regard any of these trends as necessarily terminal, but rather as serious challenges with which informed people could deal successfully through political action. I spent a good many of those years, while exerting myself as an activist, advocate and candidate, mystified about why these issues gained so little traction in the media, in politics, and in the public discourse. I have since learned why. And the knowledge has impelled me to the belief that it is too late to avert the crash of our civilization.

The Mortality of Hope

"How are you doing?" a character was asked in a novel I read a long time ago. "A lot better," was the answer, "since I gave up hope."

I submit that it is only in giving up hope for our benighted industrial civilization that we can grasp the hope that exists for us as humans. Logic and facts inexorably lead to two conclusions: that the world cannot be saved; and that we can save ourselves. There is no scenario that shows us how to convert the United States to renewable and sustainable energy, yet there is no reason that you or I, along with our families, cannot be living on renewable and sustainable energy within a few months. There is no way to provide wholesome, local food for the population of the nation; for you and me and our families, it is simply a matter of making some choices and doing some work. You and I could create a sanctuary for our families capable of sustaining even the loss of our civilization. In the worst case, our sanctuaries would replace our civilization.

An even more hopeful scenario could be held out: that if you and I, and our friends and their friends, begin to take seriously the desperate need for sustainable living, and act on it, and learn about it, and do it, we could create a critical mass of people who could shift our entire civilization toward sustainability.

But it's probably too late for that. If you are on a luxury cruise aboard a marvel of modern technology, no one is going to convince you that you should tear yourself away from the banquets and the champagne and the dancing to work frantically building a lifeboat. Then for a time, after your Titanic has hit its iceberg, it may be appropriate to work with the crew and the other passengers to try to save the ship. But there comes a time, when the bow is down and the water is rushing in and time is running out, that it is appropriate to save yourself.

That time is now. It is the end of our voyage. The end of an age.

Prologue

Every culture tells itself a story of the Fall. We all seem to have a vestigial memory of a golden age long ago when people lived in harmony with each other and with the world, and we need to reconcile that memory with the broken connections and dismal prospects of our present. We of the Judeo-Christian tradition have enshrined our best attempt to do so in our Bible, in the Genesis story of Adam and Eve's expulsion from the Garden of Eden. It is the first story about humans to appear in the scripture. It is probably the best-known Bible story, and the least well understood.

The moral of the story, as it has been simplified for children and remembered by most, is that if you do not obey God, something terrible will happen to you. God told them not to eat apples, they did anyway, and they got thrown out of their home. It is a perfect proverb for unruly teenagers and unreliable factory workers.

Not only is there more to this story, there is a totally different story hiding in plain sight.

There are at least two ways to think about the ordinances of God as delivered by scripture. For example, if God were represented as saying to you, "Take one more step and I will throw you from this cliff and dash you to your death on the rocks below," then you may be forgiven for thinking that God is a fierce and arbitrary guy, which is exactly how He seems in much of the Old Testament. But what if He is not really threatening you with retribution for disobedience, but rather warning you about the inevitable consequences of a certain action? What if He is really informing you that from where you are standing, a single step forward means falling to your death on the rocks below, under the influence of gravity (which, after all, is a law of God)? Similarly, when He says, "the wages of sin are death," he can be taken as threatening capital punishment for small trans-gressions, or as warning us about the effect of a law as immutable as gravity: the law that says if we behave badly, we cannot be happy, and we die a little. A great deal depends on the translation, the tone of the translator, and the condition of the listener.

The translator gauges his audience. If my audience is a small child with whom I am walking on a busy street, I might tell him sternly to stay on the sidewalk lest I smack him. I would speak thus not out of any desire to threaten him personally, or to punish him, but out of my calculation that his ability to comprehend the dangers of traffic was not sufficiently developed, but that he would likely understand the threat of getting smacked, and act accordingly. Years later I might rely on his understanding of the possibilities, and limit myself to advising him to be careful out there.

Is it possible, then, that when God instructed Adam and Eve about their behavior in Eden, he was not merely bullying them about eating fruit, but was warning them away from something harmful? They were very young, fresh from Creation, completely uneducated, and as such probably would not have comprehended anything more subtle than an order to stay on the sidewalk or get smacked.

But you and I are grown, and educated, and knowledgeable, and we need to know: What was the warning?

Let us return to the scene of the crime.

And the LORD God planted a garden eastward in Eden; and there he put the man whom he had formed. And out of the ground made the LORD God to grow every tree that is pleasant to the sight, and good for food; the tree of life also in the midst of the garden, and the tree of knowledge of good and evil. (Genesis 2.8-9)

Thus did we all live when we were hunter-gatherers, amid plants pleasant to the sight and good for food. We think of early humans as club-carrying cave dwellers scrabbling constantly for meat, hunted by bears, trampled by mastodons, broken by the desperate and constant labor of finding food and keeping the cave warm. In fact, hunter-gatherers required only a few hours of work a week to gather all the food they needed from their plenteous surroundings, thrived in their tightly-knit, clan-based social systems, and were no more bothered by predation than we are by, for example, the 50,000 American lives claimed each year by automobiles. Nature as they experienced it was no more "red in tooth and claw," in Tennyson's benighted phrase, than are our highways.

And the LORD God commanded the man, saying, Of every tree of the garden thou mayest freely eat: but of the tree of the knowledge of good and evil, thou shalt not eat of it: for in the day that thou eatest thereof thou shalt surely die. (Genesis 2.16-17)

There is the commandment. But is it a threat, or is it

advice? If we are to understand the language literally, as a threat, we will shortly have a big problem: having been told by the Lord God that if they do this they will die, they do it, and do not die. Does the Lord God not mean what he says? Does He make empty threats? Or is the meaning deeper in the language, requiring a more subtle understanding of what was being forbidden, and what were the consequences of disobedience?

If it was a warning, what behavior was the warning about? What were the effects of eating the fruit of the tree of the knowledge of good and evil? God did not say when He delivered His warning, but the serpent did, as he later urged Eve to do it:

And the serpent said unto the woman, Ye shall not surely die: for God doth know that in the day ye eat thereof, then your eyes shall be opened, and ye shall be as gods, knowing good and evil. (Genesis 3. 4-5)

This is much more than learning right from wrong. This is comprehension that raises one to the status of a god. But what is it? It helps to know (and I am grateful to Daniel Quinn for pointing it out) that the Genesis stories gained currency long before their incorporation into scripture, at about the time that agriculture became the occupation of much of humankind. To be a farmer, you must know what plants are good -- wheat, barley, flax -- and which are weeds. Then you tend the good plants, and kill the evil ones. You know that bees are good and wasps are evil, and you do your best to kill the latter. Cattle are good, but wolves are evil. It is not just that you decide which plants and animals you like; you assemble the good ones in fields, and you kill those you do not like. Thus do you usurp the judgment of a god, having partaken of the tree of the knowledge of good and evil.

(The Bible is hardly the only holy text to convey this warning. In the *Tao Te Ching* attributed to Lao-Tzu, verse 29 reads:

As for those who would take the whole world
To tinker as they see fit,
I observe that they never succeed:
For the world is a sacred vessel
Not made to be altered by man.
The tinker will spoil it;
Usurpers will lose it.)

The first thing that Adam and Eve did upon grasping the knowledge of good and evil was to cover their nakedness. This was not necessarily an act of decency, of having judged nakedness to be evil; it can be seen as an act of separation, a way of setting oneself apart from and above the other creatures of the world -- sort of like the crimson cape of a cardinal of the church.

Such hubris might have been understandable, even before the forbidden fruit, because God had told them upon their creation to "Be fruitful, and multiply, and replenish the earth, and subdue it: and have dominion over the fish of the sea, and over the fowl of the air, and over every living thing that moveth upon the earth." (That is the King James translation. The New Standard version of the Bible changed one word: "Be fruitful and multiply, and fill the earth and subdue it." There is a substantial difference between the idea of replenishing the earth and just filling it up.) There have always been two ways to look at the idea of one thing having dominion over another. To some it means being able to do what you want with the subject. To others, the idea of dominion carries with it a heavy responsibility for the welfare of the subject.

If there had been any ambiguity on this point for Adam and Eve before the forbidden fruit, there was none after. They girded their loins with clothing and set out to take charge, pronouncing some things to be good and other things to be evil. "Behold," said the Lord God, "the man is become as one of us, to know good and evil." (To whom, one cannot help wondering, was He speaking? What did He mean, one of us?)

23

We assume that God evicted Adam and Eve because of what they had done, but that is not what Genesis tells us. What He said in Genesis was that He was throwing Adam out "lest he put forth his hand, and take also of the tree of life, and eat, and live for ever." And when the couple was gone from the garden, God posted a guard over it, "to keep the way of the tree of life." So while God had warned Adam and Eve away from the tree of knowledge, he was even more worried about them putting their hands to the tree of life.

We now have had 10,000 years of experience with the consequences of our god-like knowledge of good and evil. We have spread the good plants over the cultivated face of the earth and have waged an unending war against the bad plants. We have bred, crossbred and manipulated the good animals and have done our best to wipe out the bad ones. We have filled the earth, and we believe we have subdued it. And we believe we have done this on God's instructions.

We tell ourselves that our story has been one of constant and unbroken progress, from animal-hide capes to wash-and-wear synthetics; from charred mastodon meat to ready-in-a-minute microwave meals; from drafty caves to four-bedroom, all-electric McMansions on two-acre estates in idyllic suburbs.

In fact, there have been many hideous interruptions in this upward march. We live on the graves of countless human civilizations that have failed and vanished -- which is to say they all died. Just in the Americas, we gape as tourists at the monumental works of the Aztecs, the Mayans and the Anasazi, missing the point that in their time they were *us,* living lives blessed by unprecedented technology, extending their dominion over the earth as never before, unable to imagine anything that could harm them.

Yet they are all gone. As we re-examine their stories with our critical faculties in place, it becomes clearer that they all vanished for a single, compelling reason: they ate out the resources available to them. They decided what was good and what was evil, they became as gods, tinkered with the world, and destroyed the natural web of life that nourished them.

Perhaps we should revisit the matter of the literal truth of God's warning in Genesis: *in the day that thou eatest thereof thou shalt surely die.* In Genesis, the span of time indicated by the word "day" is a flexible concept. The creation of the universe, and all the populations thereof, took seven "days." Perhaps, in that sense, we are still in the day in which the forbidden fruit was taken.

It is easy to dismiss the fate of the Aztecs, for example, because they were so primitive compared to us. That for much of the 15th Century Mexico City was larger than Paris, with more canals than Venice and aqueducts to rival Rome's, simply does not register with us. We have surpassed them, we think, we have extended our dominion over the earth as never before, and nothing can get in our way. To us their graves are merely curiosities that confirm how far we've come.

Draped in the mantle of our knowledge of good and evil, we set to work converting our garden to a field, the fruitful jumble of creation of which we had been a part to an ordered world of which we were in charge. In search of ever larger reserves of food we invented the plow, an efficient guillotine for the living soil, and deployed it across the planet. Then we invented the internal combustion engine and gasoline, to pull larger plows faster, and synthetic fertilizers and pesticides. We did not know until recently that all these things killed the multitudinous organisms that constituted a living organism whose life supports our own. Perhaps such ignorance, even on such a vast and deadly scale, could be forgiven if, in the light of knowledge, we changed our behavior. But we have not.

We did not know that there is only so much potable water on the planet, and that if present development trends continue we will run out. Now we do. We did not know that petroleum and coal and uranium exist in finite amounts that, however large, will be exhausted by our profligate use of them. Now we do. We did not know that what we were doing had the capacity to collapse the fisheries of the vast oceans, to warm the entire planet with myriad unforeseen consequences. Now we know, and we have not altered our behavior one whit. Most of us continue to cling to the belief that "growth" and "progress" and "development" are good, that their alternatives are evil, and that any consequences are trivial that cannot be measured in cash, now. It appears that the knowledge of good and evil we acquired from the tree in Eden, while godlike in its pretensions, fell far short of omniscience.

Now, in this ruined landscape, we are moving to a higher level of management. We are feverishly tinkering with the basic codes of creation, the awesome and mysterious genetic instructions that convert the will of the Creator to the flesh of the world. We are doing this, of course, for profit, to improve the "good" plants and animals, to cure the evil diseases that afflict us good guys, with a potential cash flow that would excite Croesus and with a cost of which we know nothing.

We have, in other words, done exactly what God said we would do after Eden: we have put forth our hands, and taken of the second tree, the Tree of Life, that we might live forever. We are beginning to comprehend the consequences of our first transgression in Eden. What the costs of this second sin will be, God only knows.

PART I: FOOD

*"In nature, there are neither rewards nor punishments;
there are consequences."*

Robert Greene Ingersoll

Chapter One: Losing Ground

I had not been back to the family wheat farm for several years, and it had been even longer since I had been there during spring planting. It was an hour's drive from the airport to the farm, not enough time for one accustomed to the embrace of mountains to get over the feelings of vertigo induced by the immense impersonal sprawl of the prairie, the sudden enormity of the sky and distance of the horizons. Machinery crawling over the black loam miles away was clearly visible, as were the sentinel grain elevators that marked the small towns. As my father and I approached the home place by car, on that day sometime in the 1980s, I saw a neighbor planting his field, his giant tractor pulling a seeder at least 40 feet wide, and something about the picture bothered me. Eventually, I got it.

"Where are the sea gulls?" I asked.

My father grunted. "Haven't seen a sea gull in years." (They weren't really sea gulls, of course, we were located about as far from the sea as it's possible to get on the North American continent. We were using the generic term for what were really Franklin's Gulls.}

"What happened to them?" I remembered that my seemingly endless hours on a tractor as a teenager had been enlivened by the tumultuous flocks that followed whatever implement I was pulling, diving and shrieking and jostling over the bounty of worms and grubs revealed by the turning of the soil.

My father shrugged. "Nothing for them to eat."

That was the end of that discussion (it was a longish one, for us). But the memory of that empty air behind our neighbor's tractor, and my father's dismissive response, remained tucked away in my mind, a tiny irritant awaiting explanation. It was years before it sprang to mind again, when as a journalist I was covering the controversy over the federal government's attempt to label organic produce. I asked a soil scientist how many laboratory tests were needed to determine that agricultural chemicals had not been used on a parcel of land for three years. He laughed.

"It's easy. You pick up a clump of dirt and see if any thing's alive in it. If there is, it passes."

I had grown up on a farm whose livelihood depended entirely on growing things in soil, and I had never known about, or attached any importance to, the things that live in soil, unless I was looking for worms to bait a fishing hook. If you had tried to tell the farmers of my youth that the health of the worms in their dirt was important to their well-being, and that the disappearance of the gulls was a dire omen, they would have laughed; had you gone on to say that the soil itself is a living organism, that a shovel full of healthy soil contains more living things than there are humans on the planet, they would have thrown a net over you.

My father was a novice farmer in 1945, when my mother inherited part of her father's farm. I have the notebooks in which he recorded his education as a modern agri-businessman. Almost every year there were new products with which to farm -- new implements, new strains of seed, and especially new chemicals. He was an eager adapter of everything the extension agents and chemical salesmen laid before him for the betterment of his kind: synthetic fertilizers, whose proponents insisted that they provided everything a plant needed, nitrogen, phosphorous and potassium, never mind the other 97 elements present in natural soil; 2,4-D, with its magical ability to ignore the good plants such as wheat and kill the evil ones -- mustard, sow thistle and the like; DDT, used not only to protect crops from insect pests but around ball parks and yards to lift the plague of mosquitoes so that people could work or take their ease of a summer evening without annoyance; the pre-emergence sprays to knock out wild oats, whose leaves resembled wheat and ignored 2,4-D; the fungicides that battled black smut and red rust. A bulky sprayer took its place in the line of implements parked behind the barn, and the vinegar smell of poison became a familiar taint on the prairie wind.

My father had no reason to think, nor did he hear any dissenting voice suggest, that he was doing anything wrong. Farming was a business, a farm was a factory, the world was a machine. You improved your business by increasing your output, enlarging your factory, or cutting your expenses (this last method was seldom emphasized by the salesmen who were the chief educators of farmers; they were not there to save farmers money). The soil was the factory floor, the place where the product was assembled, and no one suspected that it was a living organism, that just like any cow or chicken or person, it could be harmed by poisons. Dirt was dirt.

By the 1970s, the soil in our area -- an eight-foot deep layer of black loam, one of the most fertile grain-growing areas on the planet -- was so sterile the seeds you planted would not even sprout unless you injected anhydrous ammonia in the ground before seeding in the spring.

By the end of the 1970s, my cousin Jim typified the new agri-businessman. He owned and leased 5,000 acres, operated his own fertilizer plant, flew two aircraft -- one for spraying chemicals and another for travel -- maintained a fleet of huge tractors, combines and implements and presided over a small city of sheds, granaries, hangars and tanks around his house. All of this was, as the current saying goes, highly leveraged. "I live," he said to me ruefully one day, "one hailstorm away from bankruptcy."

Dirty Secrets

I came across the statistic while preparing the annual Environmental Quality Index for *National Wildlife* Magazine. It ranks among the most stunning numbers I have ever seen, and at first I simply could not believe it. But thorough checking confirmed it: Every year since the 1970s, **American farmers have lost to wind and water erosion about seven pounds of topsoil for every pound of food and fiber they have produced**. According to the National Resources Conservation Service of the US Department of Agriculture, that's the average rate: improved conservation practices lowered the rate of loss from eight pounds of soil per pound of yield in the 1970s to six pounds per pound in the 1990s. In general, Asia is losing topsoil at twice the US rate and China at triple the US rate. 1

According to a 2006 study by David Pimentel, professor of ecology at Cornell University, the United States continues to lose topsoil 10 times faster than it can be replenished. China and India are losing theirs at 30 to 40 times the replenishment rate. The soil, he notes, is the source of 99.7% of the world's food (the remainder is found in oceans, lakes and rivers) and we are losing 37,000 square miles of ground *every year*. During the past 40 years, 30% of the world's arable land has disappeared while the population

---

1 *Summary Report 1992 National Resources Inventory,* US Soil Conservation Service (as it was then called), Washington DC 1994. *Land Degradation,* C.J. Barrow. Cambridge University Press 1991.

doubled, from about 3.3 billion in 1965 to 7 billion in 2012.[2]

The mind boggles. For nearly half a century the Farm Bureaus and Archer-Daniels-Midlands and chambers of commerce have been raving about the productivity of the American farmer while all that time every ton of grain in the bin cost *seven tons* of topsoil. Comprehending that fact produced in me the first twinges of doubt that we could save ourselves. If we are greedy enough knowingly to destroy the source of almost all our food for quick profit, what hope could there be for us?

Water brings soil into our life, by wearing down mountains and, in the form of ice, splitting rocks. And if it is given a chance water will take that soil right back out of our life. According to the Pimentel study, one rainstorm can strip more than five tons of topsoil from an acre of plowed ground not protected by plants. Natural soil formation -- the slow work of worms, fungi, bacteria, amoeba, nematodes, mites and moles, digesting the husks of plants and the corpses of insects and the occasional animal, processing and rearranging the minerals, mixing them with organic content and aerating the whole while establishing tiny irrigation canals carrying water to the depths and returning trace minerals to the surface -- could replace the soil lost in a single rainstorm in about 20 years if left to work undisturbed. (Those critical subterranean activities, collectively called bioturbation, were noticed by Charles Darwin but not named until the 1950s and did not become central to our understanding of soil and its formation until the 1990s.)

Then there is the wind.

I remember the dust storms of my childhood, remember watching them approach like thunderstorms fallen from the sky to crawl along the ground, black towering clouds erupting from the earth. I remember days with the sun muted to twilight at noon, the howling wind vibrating the wood shingles on our roof so that they made a growling whine, gray powder insinuating itself into the

---

2 Pimentel, David. "Soil Erosion, A Food and Environmental Threat *," Journal of the Environment, Development and Sustainability,* Vol. 8 No.1/Feb. 2006

house, coating the shelves and counters and tables, leaving silhouettes of our heads on the pillows, grating constantly in our teeth.

No, it was not the Dust Bowl, it was 20 years later and a thousand miles away. The two persistent myths about the Dust Bowl are that it was caused by drought, and that it is over.

We did not know that it was our dying soil that was in the wind. We knew that our days-long events of the 1950s were not nearly as bad or as frequent as the weeks-long dust storms of the Dust Bowl days. We knew about the Dust Bowl because we had read and had been taught about it. But we had not read, nor been taught, about the conclusion of the US Soil Conservation Service *at the time* that the Dust Bowl was not a natural disaster, but a man-made event. It wasn't the drought that created the dust, it was the plow. Undisturbed grassland does not blow away, no matter how dry it gets, it just hunkers down and waits for rain. Plowed ground leaves.

The plow has long been revered as the first agricultural technology, the machine that made us productive and wealthy. It turns out, instead, that the plow was the guillotine that executed the living soil. We did not know that every foot the blade of the plow travels, it severs millions of minute, complex interconnections between the surface and the bedrock by way of which myriad materials -- water, air, trace minerals, nutrients -- are distributed through the soil to where they are needed. We thought we had to plow, to "loosen" the soil, learning only belatedly that repeated plowing creates a concrete-like hardpan at the level of its lowest reach that is impervious to water, roots, and microbes. Meanwhile the loosened soil above, severed from its nourishment, naked to sun, wind and water, dies and when it is not covered by vegetation, blows away.

The first plows were pulled by people. Oxen and other beasts of burden increased a farmer's reach from several acres to dozens of acres (40 acres and a mule were considered by the Federal government a sufficient homestead for a black family freed as a consequence of the Civil War). But the oil-fueled internal combustion engine enabled a single farmer to execute thousands of acres of good ground.

The plow is far from the only weapon that kills the soil, it was merely the first. Its steel offspring -- cultivators, rod weeders, discers, and the like -- also obliterate life when overused. But it was the onset of chemical warfare that sealed the fate of the soil.

Fruit of the Poison Tree

For the first 9,800 years or so of the 10,000-year history of agriculture, we used our knowledge of good and evil to maneuver more or less within the parameters that nature gave us. We facilitated the breeding of the good plants and animals to get more of what we wanted -- faster maturation, more resistance to drought, disease and insects, and greater yields. To counter the inevitable exhaustion of what were called "old fields," we rotated crops, used companion planting, rested fields for a season ("summer fallow," we called it) applied animal manures and such things as bone meal, ashes and seaweed to maintain fertility. In all of this we acted as nature's assistant, observing closely to see what she did and then using our judgment and labor to do more of the same.

But in the 19th Century, increasingly restive to be mere assistants, we began taking over active management of the processes of creation. The hubris was expressed by one of the inventors of fertilizer -- the Hessian chemist Justus von Liebig -- in the form of what could reasonably be regarded either as a profound principle of science or a profound heresy: Von Liebig believed that life consisted of nothing more than chemical processes, and that between the chemical processes of the living and those of the dead there was no difference. The spiritual ramifications of such a belief are stupendous, but were studiously ignored then as they are now in the name of objective science.

If life is simply a series of chemical reactions, exactly like those that result in, for example, plastic, then it is within the scope of human comprehension. All that is required to understand life, hence to manage and even to create it, is to learn its set of equations. The list may be long, and we may not know it entirely yet, but it is *knowable*. And when we know it, we will have the power. (Cue the maniacal laugh of the mad scientist of the stock horror movie, bent on taking over the world. There is a reason that he is such a dominant and endlessly recurring theme of popular entertainment.)

The source of von Liebig's hubris, and the reason for his coronation as "the father of fertilizer," was his conclusion in the mid-19th Century that what plants needed to flourish was certainly not a living soil -- he scoffed at humus -- but a handful of compounds and minerals. The most important of these, he found, was nitrogen: not the gas that makes up most of the atmosphere, but nitrogen in compounds that can be used by plants. He devised a way to capture free nitrogen in the form of ammonia by treating bone meal with sulfuric acid, but could not convince any plant to partake of what he had made. It was as if a scientist had concluded that the most important things mothers do was nurse and hug their babies; had devised a machine that periodically sprayed the babies with milk and squeezed them; and wondered why the babies thus mothered did not thrive.

The example was meant to be silly but it's not so far from the truth according to von Liebig. As he identified nitrogen and a few other things as the only nourishment needed by plants, so he declared protein, fat and carbohydrates, plus a couple of minerals, to be sufficient nutrition for humans. Among these few substances, he regarded protein as the "master nutrient," for humans just as nitrogen was for plants. He demonstrated his theories by devising the world's first baby formula, leaving him and his followers to wonder why the babies thus nourished did not thrive. Thus von Liebig turns out to be not only the father of chemical-industrial agriculture, which has destroyed the soil on which it depends, but the father as well of what Michael Pollan calls the nutritionist movement that has managed to make a

dismaying   proportion   of   Americans   overweight   and
undernourished at the same time.3

His failures to synthetically nourish either babies or plants
did nothing to reduce von Liebig's reputation as a man whose
theories -- that the soil was dead, that its humus, or organic
content, was irrelevant to plant health, and that any nutrients the
plant needed could be replicated by chemistry -- defined the future
of agriculture.

While the world awaited the refinement of chemical agriculture, it witnessed the onset of industrial agriculture.

Enough is Not Enough

The first purpose of industrial agriculture is to lift the limits
imposed by the carrying capacities of natural systems. An
ecosystem that is in balance stays there by limiting the number of
its guests. Most of us carry in our heads primitive notions about
how nature imposes these limits, involving bloody predation and
ghastly famines that cut populations to the bone. In fact, nature is
usually far more subtle and a good deal more gentle. For example:
female mammals in the wild typically will not conceive if their
body fat is low. They don't have to say, "I just don't want to bring a
child into a world where food is scarce." Their bodies decide when
times are hard, without discussion, and react accordingly.
Similarly, a contracting food supply does not necessarily mean
mass famine. Instead, some of the elderly and seriously ill may
pass a week or a month before they otherwise would have; here
and there a marginally weak infant will not survive. By this and
many other such strategies, animals and people who live in their
surroundings in such a way as to be governed by natural laws
seldom encounter drastic adversity.

In the past, one of the absolute limits on the productivity of
farm fields was set by the availability of nitrogen. Although it
makes up 80 per cent of the atmosphere, in its free gaseous form it

---

3Pollan, Michael. *In Defense of Food.* New York: Penguin Press 2008 is of no use to plants. It must first be "fixed," joined with another element in a compound that plants can take up. Joined with hydrogen, for example, it forms ammonia, which higher organisms can use to form such essentials of life as proteins, or chlorophyll, or amino acids, or nucleic acids. [I had to struggle, just there, to avoid writing "building blocks of life," one of those phrases that condition us to think of the world in simplistic, mechanistic terms.]

In nature, the primary fixers of nitrogen are legumes -- or, to be precise, the bacteria that live in nodes on the roots of legumes. Grain crops are heavy consumers of soil nitrogen. Corn is the worst, taking up a half-ton per acre or so during its growing season. Farmers (the term is used here to distinguish from industrial agri-businessmen) used to plant legumes after corn to replace nitrogen and to cover and protect the soil from erosion, and they applied manure from their animals to add even more. They were thus limited to using perhaps half their land (the part not grazed or hayed for their livestock), less than half the time (two years in five was regarded as the maximum for corn) for grain production. Industrial agriculture regards all such limitations as evil, and works to eliminate them.

Among the first of many differences to emerge between farmers and hunter-gatherers was that the farmer stored and defended surpluses, so that there would never be a season in which my lady's body fat was low. It turned out, of course, that surpluses can not only be held against future shortages, but transported from high-carrying-capacity areas (or countries or continents) to low ones. On another hand, if the carrying capacity of one area is limited by the availability of water, the building of aqueducts, canals and dams can remove that limitation. By such means do we seek to suspend natural limits, which are as basic to biology as gravity is to physics.

People go on airplane flights that, by climbing and then putting the nose down at a certain velocity, give the experience of weightlessness to the passengers. Thus is the law of gravity apparently suspended for a time, giving the passengers a few seconds to float free, and live their dreams of weightlessness. Then it's over -- because of course they did not suspend the law, they just fiddled around its edges -- and if the passengers are not ready for it, the sudden return of the law will bang them up pretty thoroughly.

You're Sh***ing Me

As early farmers worked to produce larger surpluses, to move water over longer distances, to bring more land under cultivation and to cultivate what they had more effectively, the scope of their activities increased relentlessly. One of the earliest agricultural activities to become both industrial and global in scale was the application of fertilizer. Not the synthetic fertilizers imagined by von Liebig and others, not at first. One of the first global agribusiness products in the world (and one that has very much come back into favor) was bird shit.

All right, guano. Not from just any bird, but from birds that eat fish. Not from just any place, but one where little rain falls on the guano to leach away the nutrients in it, where few plants grow to take up the nutrients, and where large numbers of the right birds congregate regularly to deposit significant amounts. The best places on earth are a series of tiny, barren, rocky islands off the coast of Peru. Indigenous people had been using the stuff on their crops since the dawn of time, and it was a habit noted by European visitors who, as was their wont, not only adapted the practice but figured out how to make fortunes from it.

English traders established a monopoly on bird crap collected in the Peruvian islands, and in every year of the second half of the 19th Century shipped five million tons of the stuff to Europe. American and other European traders began to claim various guano islands in the Caribbean and elsewhere in the Pacific, while still others discovered that bat guano, protected from weathering and plants in dry caves, worked almost as well. Thus did agriculture in several countries become dependent, for the first time, on an expensive commodity that had to be transported great distances before it could be used. 4

Meanwhile others were clawing at the tree of life to see what chemicals nourished it. Germany's von Liebig, Sir John Bennet Lawes of England, Jean-Baptiste Boussingault in France, Erling Johnson of Norway and others were asking the question: what do plants want? Their collective answer: nitrogen, phosphorous and potassium, which became known by their chemical abbreviations as N, P and K. The problem, as von Liebig demonstrated by not solving it, was to formulate the nutrients in a form plants could use.

The Humanitarian

Enter one of history's more equivocal actors, Fritz Haber. An extremely patriotic German chemist, Haber liberated his country from its dependence on saltpeter for the manufacture of munitions. Saltpeter, sodium nitrate, is a naturally occurring nitrogen compound that was available in industrial quantities virtually only from Chile, thus posing a security issue for Germany that would become acute during its prosecution of World War I. Before that war began, Haber, along with his associate Carl Bosch, found a way to use nitrogen from the atmosphere to make ammonia, a compound of nitrogen and hydrogen that did as well as saltpeter in the manufacture of explosives. Moreover, this synthetic ammonia, unlike von Liebig's product, worked fine as a fertilizer. With the raw materials, nitrogen and hydrogen, readily available in unlimited quantities (nitrogen from the air, hydrogen from petroleum or natural gas) and with the source of energy to process it, electricity, almost as cheap and plentiful as the ingredients, the dawn of unlimited industrial agriculture was at hand. 5

Not content to be a pioneer in the manufacture of conventional munitions, Haber enthusiastically advocated the deployment

---

4 Trade and Environment Database: http://www.american.edu/TED/guano.htm
5 Roberts, Paul. *The End of Food*. Boston: Houghton Mifflin 2008, p.21

of chemical weapons on the battlefields of World War I. To the strenuous moral objections raised by German military officers (and his own wife Clara, an accomplished chemist) Haber responded that "death is death," thus adding to von Liebig's assertion that there is no chemical distinction between the living and the dead a corollary: there is no meaningful distinction to be made among manners of death. Haber devised a way to poison enemy soldiers with chlorine gas and personally oversaw its inaugural use at the Second Battle of Ypres on April 22, 1915. Three weeks later his distraught wife committed suicide. Hours after she died, Haber left for the Russian front to try his gas warfare again.

After the Great War, Haber was awarded the Nobel Prize for chemistry for his achievement in synthesizing ammonia. The Nobel committee emphasized, of course, its gift of fertilizer for feeding people, rather than of ammunition for killing them. But neither his achievements, nor his honors nor his diseased patriotism was sufficient to protect him when Hitler's minions discovered that his parents had been Jews (Haber had converted to Christianity in a futile attempt to blend). He had to go into exile to avoid becoming a guest of a concentration camp, and while there perhaps a consumer of another product he developed -- the insecticide and humanicide Zyklon B, the preferred poison gas of Nazi death-camp managers.

The problem with Fritz Haber, one of his biographers, Margit Szöllösi-Janze, told National Public Radio, is that people don't know whether to admire him, or despise him. "On the one hand, you have the inventor of ammonia synthesis -- the benefactor of humanity. On the other, you have the gas warrior, the terrible husband, who drove his wife to commit suicide. We tend toward this polarization, and we don't see as much as we should, that these two things belong together. It's the same science and the same person, doing both." Indeed. And when the bookkeeping is complete, it may well be that the human toll in death and suffering exacted by fertilizer, thanks to this "benefactor," will far exceed that inflicted by chemical weapons (which in fact never worked very well on the battlefield), and all the casualties of conventional munitions as well. 6

On the debit side of the books already is the enormous harm done by nitrogen compounds that run off farm fields (and lawns and golf courses) because plants cannot absorb the huge doses of synthetics that are typically administered. Manufacturers' recommended application rates are self-servingly inflated, and agri-businessmen typically use them as minimums in a belief that if a little bit works, much more will work much better. Nitrates that leach into drinking water pose a serious health threat, especially to the young. The compounds interfere with the ability of infants' blood to carry oxygen, one of the effects of which (in addition to diarrhea, vomiting, difficulty in breathing and failure to thrive) is a blue tinge to the skin: hence the label "Blue Baby Disease." Synthetic fertilizer has become a major and growing source of nitrous oxide, a potent greenhouse gas (that is, one of the gases that acts to trap the sun's heat in the lower atmosphere, thus raising the temperature at the surface) and destroyer of the upper ozone layer (that shields the surface from harmful ultraviolet radiation). 7

But it is as a nutrient, not as a poison, that nitrates pose their most pervasive threat. In streams, rivers and lakes, they stimulate the growth of primitive plants called algae, often so much that the vegetation forms a thick mat on the surface of the water that blocks sunlight, killing underwater vegetation, starving out the insect life and eventually the fish. When the algae die, their decomposition uses all the oxygen in the water, so that anything still alive and unable to leave the area, suffocates. The runoff from every fertilized field, every chemical-soaked lawn and golf course, and the output of every sewage treatment plant adds its load of nitrates, the dosage increasing steadily as you go down any stream. As a result, at the mouths of our great rivers, for example in the

---

6 http://www.npr.org/programs/morning/features/2002/jul/fritzhaber/
7 http://www.igac.noaa.gov/newsletter/highlights/1998/n2o.php

Gulf of Mexico and the Chesapeake Bay, are vast areas called dead zones, where nothing lives. The United Nations reported in 2003 that there were 150 such dead zones around the world. In the summer of 2008, the dead zone off the mouth of the Mississippi River extended over 8,000 square miles. Moreover, artificially stimulated algal blooms, known colloquially as "red tides," afflict shores around the world not only by depriving the water of its oxygen, but in the case of some varieties of algae, adding to it a powerful toxin.

The current fad is to discuss our "carbon footprint" -- our generation of carbon dioxide and its effect on global warming. But our nitrogen footprint has an equal potential to accomplish our destruction.

The Chemical Reaction

At the beginning of the age of fertilizer, however, the only consequences that anyone foresaw were increased yields, ever more prosperity and no more worries about depleted land. The first aftereffects to set in were regarded as good problems to have, with technological solutions readily at hand. One was that the fertilizer stimulated the growth not only of the good grains, but of the evil weeds. The answer was to develop more potent herbicides that quickly became widely deployed. In addition, the increasing acreage of single-variety crops led inevitably (we now know) to a burgeoning of the insects that like to feed on that particular crop. The answer was to drench the crop in pesticides.

All this gave farmers a terrific sense of well being. Chemicals increased yields, although almost all the proceeds from the larger harvests seemed to end up in the accounts of the chemical companies. The answer was to bring more acres under cultivation, and the machinery manufacturers cooperated by devising larger machines -- tractors the size of houses, sprayers with booms that seemed to stretch to the horizon. The farmer that bought or leased the additional land and bought the bigger equipment was, of course, up to his neck in debt, not only to the banks and finance companies but to the fuel suppliers and the tax man. Hence my cousin's remark about living one thunderstorm away from bankruptcy.

Prices for the farmers' products, meanwhile, were in the iron grip of implacable global markets in which the farmer had no negotiating power: my father hoped for $2-a-bushel wheat from the time he started farming in the 1940s (the US farm price in 1945 was $1.49) until he gave it up, a poor old man, in the 1990s when the price (in 1998) was $2.65 -- about 30 cents in 1945 money. (A perennially popular joke among farmers quotes a 90-year old farmer who won a multi-million-dollar lottery jackpot as saying, when asked what he was going to do with the money: "Oh, I reckon I'll just keep farming until it's gone.")

With absolutely no ironic intent, the period when the industrialization of agriculture hit its stride in the mid-20th Century is called the Green Revolution. The name green as used here has nothing to do, as it does now, with methods that are sustainable or at least minimally harmful to the environment. It refers to the period of intensive plant breeding, chemical development, and irrigation projects that spread across the world beginning in the mid-1940s (accelerated in the United States by the conversion in 1947, for example, of the enormous munitions plant at Muscle Shoals, Alabama to the manufacture of fertilizer)[8], and by the mid-1980s had more than doubled cereal grain production in the developing world.[9] (In the late 1980s, however, the entire effort collapsed in Africa and began to decline elsewhere.) It was this agricultural revolution in agriculture -- say the lords of agribusiness at every opportunity -- that enabled food production to keep pace with world population growth. [10]

It was also, of course, the thing that enabled the growth of

---

8 Pollan, Michael *The Omnivore's Dilemma* p. 41
9 Conway, Gordon. *The Doubly Green Revolution*. Ithaca: Cornell University Press, 1998
10 Roberts, *The End of Food* pp. 150-52

global chemical companies, global food processors, global machinery manufacturers and global finance. If your only values are those of industrialization, you like almost everyone will accept that the green revolution was good for humanity because it kept up with the increase in human numbers. But those whose values are rooted in nature, in the balance of natural systems, see it differently. The Green Revolution *enabled* explosive world population growth, which it cannot now sustain. The correction of this artificially stimulated overpopulation -- whether triggered by climate change, oil shortages, the disappearance of topsoil, something else or all of the above -- promises to be apocalyptic. To congratulate agribusiness for keeping up with world population is like congratulating a team of firefighters for trying to save a house from a fire they set.

The Bigger, the Bigger

The argument that propels the industrialization of everything, agriculture included, is that as any operation gets bigger, it realizes more and more economies of scale. The more you make or grow, this theory says, the less each unit or bushel will cost, and the more profit you will make on each. What this notion ignores is that the economies-of-scale theory has a dark twin: concentration of risk. Nature limits the size and number of its constituents, but not their diversity. To the extent we do the opposite, increase numbers and size while decreasing diversity, we increase our risk. The choice is between long-term survival (nature's way) and short-term money. The money has been winning for a very long time.

As the small, diversified farms of yesterday have been replaced by the huge, monoculture factories of today, both the risk of failure, and the size of any failure, have increased dramatically. Yesterday, if your pigs got sick and died you cleaned out the sty and still had the chickens and the cows; in today's pig "factory," 50,000 pigs contract an antibiotic-resistant illness and the repercussions are continental in scale. Yesterday, if a fungus got your wheat, chances are you still had your corn and oats and hay; today, a wheat-loving bug, fungus or disease, loose in your 5,000 acres of only wheat, can take you down.

No one seems to have noticed that the economies of scale have never worked for agriculture. A tractor dealer in Iowa, the heart of American agri-business, told *Mother Jones* Magazine recently, "No one is making money around here. In a good year, farmers can expect to invest $320 an acre for a harvest worth $350 an acre." Without government subsidies, most growers would be gone. American agriculture, which sees itself as a triumph of American self-reliance and free enterprise, is to an astonishing degree a socialist undertaking.

Meanwhile the ill effects of industrialized agriculture -- studiously ignored by those enriched by it, aggressively played down by the publicists and politicians in its employ -- have swelled slowly but inexorably over a half century to their present tsunami-like proportions. The dead soils blew and washed away, the tainted waters mingled, increasingly strangling life in rivers lakes and estuaries, the chemical fogs thickened and extended while the oil-guzzling machinery of production and distribution belched their pollutants into the air, and almost everywhere on the planet subsistence agriculture -- diverse, sustainable, feeding its practitioners first -- was replaced with single-plant, large-scale industrial agriculture that could not get through a year without huge quantities of imported machinery, petroleum, fertilizer, pesticides, money -- and food for the farmers. (Food author Michael Pollan writes compellingly of his epiphany, on a visit to the most productive agricultural region in the world, the American Midwest. He was, he realized, in a food desert, where everything produced to "feed the world," as agribusiness likes to say, was whisked away to be processed into food-like substances.[11] These farmers' food, like everyone else's, travels on average a thousand miles and more to

---

11 Pollan, Michael, *Omnivore's Dilemma: A Natural History of Four Meals.* New York, The Penguin Press 2006

get to their tables. If anything goes wrong, they will be among the first to starve.[12]

To Hug a Tree

Public resistance to this carnage has grown very slowly, in the face of its perpetrators' extravagant cash payoffs to those who influence communications and politics. Rachel Carson's 1962 book *Silent Spring*, which detailed the catastrophic effects of the use of DDT, helped ignite what has come to be known as the environmental movement in the United States. Seven years later the super-polluted Cuyahoga River became the movement's poster child when it caught fire (yes, I know, it was oily gunk floating in the water that caught fire, but the river looked like it was burning and that picture was worth a lot more than the customary thousand words).

The movement enjoyed a few successes. DDT was banned, with one emblematic result being that the bald eagle was saved from extinction. The Cuyahoga was cleansed of its most visible gunk, after which riverside restaurants and development reinvigorated the city of Cleveland. Lead was removed from paint and gasoline after taking a terrible toll on the developing brains of children exposed to it. When the Freon that was in everybody's air conditioners was identified as the principal agent that was destroying the high-altitude ozone layer, thus exposing earthlings to overdoses of ultraviolet radiation, Freon was banned -- and the ozone layer actually repaired itself.

There was a time, in the 1980s, when it was possible to believe that the culture was changing, that we were on the way to figuring out how to live in a less damaging way. Movie stars took up the cause, the Saturday cartoons for kids featured polluters and developers as villains, organizations dedicated to wildlife and ecosystems flourished, organic food and recycling became stylish,

---

12 The oft-quoted number of 1500 miles has been criticized because the 2001 study that produced it (by Rich Pirog of Iowa State University's Leopold Center for Sustainable Agriculture) considered only American-grown produce.

and we waited expectantly for the political and economic spheres to capitulate to the new sensibilities.

They not capitulate, they accelerated the destruction. Industrial agriculture used its cash to coat itself in greenwash (fraudulent advertising claiming environmental stewardship where none existed), to elect sympathetic politicians (*see Chapter Five, The Failed State*), and to market and disguise its chemical products. Their greatest public-relations achievement, which persists to this day, was to define "environmentalism" as a special interest, practiced by "environmentalists" who thereafter had to compete in the marketplace of ideas on an equal footing with other special interests such as coal mining companies, electric utilities, chemical manufacturers and the like. Once this was established, any journalist covering, for example, the danger posed to groundwater quality and supply by a huge factory-farm operation, would quote the objections of "environmentalists" and then balance them with industry or chamber-of-commerce spokespeople. Thus were those concerned about the survival of humankind squeezed into slots the same size as those worried about their profits. It was, and remains, a great victory for the forces of greed.

In addition, industrialists learned in the 1990s that with a sufficiently large advertising budget, they need not worry about telling the truth. If they advertised a sugar-coated cereal as nutritious, showing happy mothers watching gluttonous children wolf it down, many times a day across the television bandwidth, then it simply did not matter that some scientist on an occasional TV show or panel discussion pointed out that the cereal consisted of empty calories that promoted tooth decay, obesity and diabetes. Given enough repetition, BS beats brains every time. It was a small mutation in the practice of advertising, which for at least 40 years had operated on the principle that if you tell people often enough that they need something, pretty soon they need it. But just as a tiny mutation can turn a virus from a minor irritant into a killer, this change had deadly ramifications.

Genetic Mutilation

With their opponents out-spent and marginalized, the agricultural-industrial complex took us all on a quantum leap into a new, and infinitely more risky gamble with the web of life. It was as if, having eaten their fill of the fruit of the tree of knowledge, they enacted the worst-case scenario depicted in Genesis at the end of the story of the Fall: they put their hands on the Tree of Life itself. They began to play Russian Roulette with the very codes of creation.

They called it genetic manipulation, giving it a name that implied they knew what they were doing. As we shall see, they did not, do not and cannot.

The codes of creation -- the instructions that tell a cell how to become a complex organism -- are contained in a substance, an acid, called deoxyribonucleic acid, or DNA. In living cells, DNA exists in chromosomes, pairs of elongated, strand-like molecules that twine around each other to form a double helix, like a spiral staircase, each strand linked to the other by a series of links that resemble steps, called base pairs. But what a staircase! Chromosome number one of the 24 that make up the human genome has 220 million steps. In all, there are something like 3.1 billion base pairs in the human genome, which is not appreciably larger or more complicated than, say, that of a flatworm.

When a cell reproduces, its chromosomes disconnect all the billions of base pairs connecting the spiral molecules -- think of a huge spiral staircase dissolving at the center of the stairs -- after which each half of the chromosome creates a mirror image of itself, and when that image has materialized into reality connects to it, and as a new chromosome goes to its new cell carrying all the instructions for creating all the cells of its organism, and for governing all the biochemical processes on which the life of that organism will depend.

People lie in the grass on a summer night, gazing at the

splendid infinity of the macro-universe above them, and respond with profound awe to the incomprehensible majesty of creation. Confronted with equal -- and equally unknowable -- complexity and mystery at the micro level, we reach for hammers and tongs to see if we can improve it.

Sections of the staircase/chromosome have been identified as affecting specific parts or processes of the organism. These sections are called genes. As usual, scientists had no more than discovered some of these connections when they set out to tinker with them. They found that certain enzymes (catalysts that cause or speed up biochemical processes) had the effect of cutting certain genes from the chromosome, and that other enzymes could recombine the genes in new, man-made sequences. These sequences can act as viral vectors, infecting a cell and inserting themselves into its DNA.

The possibilities seem endless. For example, because tomatoes are sensitive to frost, their growing season is relatively short. Fish, on the other hand, can survive in very cold water. Scientists identified a gene that enables a flounder to resist cold and inserted the gene into a tomato plant, which thereafter could resist frost.

In the 1970s, Monsanto patented and successfully brought to market a new glyphosate herbicide called Roundup. It killed all growing plants, but was presented as environmentally beneficial because unlike many other ag chemicals, such as 2,4-D, it rapidly broke down and became inert after application. Twenty years later, Monsanto genetic engineers presented their masters with soybeans that had been genetically modified to be immune to Roundup. The company rolled out a huge -- and hugely successful -- marketing campaign designed to persuade farmers around the world to pay a premium price for the GM seeds, so they could stop cultivating their crops to control weeds and simply drench them with Roundup. This, Monsanto promised, would lower their costs and improve their yields. In rapid succession, Monsanto introduced herbicide-resistant varieties of corn, cotton and canola.

In fact, almost without exception, GM farming proved more expensive and produced lower yields. In 2006, the US Department of Agriculture reported that "GM crops do not increase yield potential." A 2004 UN report said that "GM crops can have reduced yields" and another, 2008 UN report, the work of more than 400 scientists around the world, concluded that genetically engineered crops "will not play a substantial role in addressing the key problems of climate change, biodiversity loss, hunger, and poverty."[13] But the results (shouted down as they were by the advertising and public relations departments of Monsanto and the other chemical companies) did nothing to slow the adoption of the new! improved! agriculture. By 2006, a decade after the genesis of Roundup-Ready crops, they occupied nearly half -- 135 million of 293 million acres -- of the cultivated cropland in the United States. [14] Monsanto's glyphosate became the most profitable agricultural chemical in history, with an average of 90-million pounds being applied to farm fields, and an additional 8 million pounds to lawns and gardens, every year. [15]

If nature is on the one hand somewhat stingy, in placing limits on the number of individual plants or animals that can live sustainably in an ecosystem, it is on the other hand lavish with respect to diversity. Nature shuns monotony and encourages explosive variety, with the result that wherever there is life, there exists not only an astonishing variety of species but of characteristics within species. Therefore, when a mortal enemy of a species appears -- whether it's another species that eats it or a man-made chemical that kills it -- however deadly the enemy may be to most, it is never deadly to all. There will always be survivors who possess immunity, and who pass that immunity to their descendants, and restore their species. So it was with Roundup.

13 http://www.americanchronicle.com/articles/76685
14 *Who Benefits from GM Crops? The Rise in Pesticide Use.* Amsterdam, January 2008. Friends of the Earth
15 US EPA 2000-2001 Pesticide Market Estimates

In just four years, the first Roundup-Resistant weeds appeared in the Roundup-Ready crops. In ten years, eight species of resistant weeds had been documented in more than 3,000 fields in 19 states. The resistant weeds could still be killed but it took much heavier applications of the chemical, which ensured that more weeds would develop more resistance. Instead of reducing the use of herbicides, which was one of the main arguments for Roundup-Ready crops, they required increased use. If the trend continues, obviously the weeds will eventually become so resistant to glyphosate that its application will no longer make sense. And there is no similar herbicide to replace it. Already, beleaguered farmers are reverting to the toxic and carcinogenic chemicals that Roundup was supposed to have replaced. 16

By deploying their enormous profits from the combination of genetic modification and chemical application, Monsanto and its colleagues -- Bayer, Pioneer, Calgene and the like -- managed to overwhelm criticism and expand relentlessly the use of genetically modified crops. The only issue that gave them some trouble (more in Europe than anywhere else) was the question of whether genetically modified or cloned crops and animals were safe to eat. Opponents decried what they called "Frankenfoods," and in some cases managed to delay official approval of certain crops for human consumption, but aside from the fact that the long-term effects of consuming these products are completely unknown, and aside from the occasional unexpected food-allergy trigger, there is no evidence that their consumption poses a danger to human health.

It's the wrong argument to have. They don't endanger the health of individual humans as much as they threaten the future of the human race.

The insertion of genes into the DNA of another organism, always described by scientists and journalists as if it is a surgically

16 http://www.sourcewatch.org/index.php?title=Monsanto_and_the_Roundup_Ready_Controversy

precise process, is in fact a crap shoot. Where the gene ends up in the chromosome of the receiving cell is essentially the product of random chance, not the intent of the perpetrators. The possibilities of creating a mutation with unforeseen properties, or of compromising the organism's ability to survive, or of unleashing some new behavior against which nothing in the world has evolved defenses, are as real as the chances the experiment will go as hoped. [17]

The scientific establishment has been unanimous in its agreement and meticulous in its methods to make sure that space travel does not lead to accidental contamination of other planets, or of our own. Concern that some microorganism, picked up from an alien system, might explode on earth with deadly effect, infuses everything humans do in space. The return of moon rocks to earth was attended by extraordinary bio-security until they were known, beyond a shadow of doubt, to be free of any imaginable contamination. The concern was later verified when salmonella bacteria carried on a 12-day flight of the space shuttle in 2006 tripled their virulence.[18] Yet for 20 years, corporate scientists have been fiddling with the codes of creation, happily creating *and releasing into the world* organisms as alien to this biosphere as anything to be found on Mars.

The world greatly -- and rightly -- fears a global pandemic that would ensue from a simple mutation of the virus that causes avian flu. Yet genetic engineers happily -- daily -- manipulate the vectors with which they transfer genes. *Those vectors are viruses.* As it is, they do not work entirely at their masters' behest. The engineers can be sure which gene they snipped, and from where, but as to where it gets inserted in the new engineered chromosome, they have no idea. It's a random event.

Our supposed competency in this field, let alone mastery, is illusory. The human genome project, the largest international

---

17 http://www.safe-food.org/-issue/dangers.html
18 BBC News: http://news.bbc.co.uk/2/hi/science/nature/7011828.stm

scientific collaboration in history, spent $3 billion over 13 years to map the human genome, which involved assigning letters to the base pairs and recording the known functions of the genes. They pronounced their mission accomplished in 2003, and declared the genome "mapped." To read this map -- that is, to say aloud the letters identifying the base pairs, one per second, 24 hours per day -- would take a hundred years. Several large companies, such as Genentech, Cetus, Biogen and Cetus, amassed billions of dollars in capital to pursue the possibilities they foresaw for manipulating the mapped genes, from curing cancer to pre-engineering children-to-order. Only after the raucous acclaim (largely self-generated) died down, did certain inconvenient facts assert themselves.

It turns out that tens of millions of base pairs in the central regions of the chromosomes are too difficult to sequence "with current technology" (the phrase in quotes being the standard disclaimer of the scientist who is already writing his next grant application). Similarly, the ends of the chromosomes -- all the ends of all the chromosomes -- could not be analyzed. So forget the middles and the ends. Then there were a few dozen, um, gaps elsewhere. Here and there. But hey, they got 92% of those suckers nailed. And that would be a towering accomplishment were it not for the fact that 97% of the identified genes are labeled -- by the scientists who so laboriously identified them -- as "junk" genes. They may be mapped, but we have no idea what they do. It is as if a team of cartographers had unveiled a state-of-the-art map of the United States, with details provided only for Rhode Island, the rest of the states represented by their names alone.

Deepak Chopra tells the story of one of his fellow MDs who was taking part in another misguided application of science, the "mapping" of the brain. This effort, a triumph for the world-as-machine viewpoint, assumes that the brain is a machine made up of buttons and levers that, when activated, perform specific tasks. Like von Liebig, the father of fertilizer, these researchers believe that life is nothing but chemistry. The doctor in Chopra's story was stimulating the area of his subject's brain that seemed to control his arm. A tiny jolt of electricity to the spot, and the man's right arm came up. Again and again. The man was conscious and watching, and when the doctor remarked that the arm was responding unfailingly to the stimulus, the subject agreed. Then the doctor asked the man if he could stop the arm from coming up. And the man did. He made a decision, and after that the little jolt of electricity never raised his arm again. The brain is not a machine, it is an organism, with infinite options, redundancies, and processes that proceed under the influence of a will that cannot be seen or sensed, let alone mapped. The same is true of the human genome.

One of the participants in the humane genome project told National Public Radio a few years after its completion that the researchers had thought that all they had to do was transcribe the alphabet of the genome to understand what it was doing. Instead, they found as they proceeded that they were in fact recording an alphabet while observing the functioning of a subtle language of which they knew nothing. It was as though scientists had celebrated the transcription of all the hieroglyphs from some ancient tomb, brandishing them in an ordered list with no clue about what they represented.

The more geneticists learn, the less they know. A specific gene, it turns out, does not produce a specific protein. It might, responding to cues or instructions whose nature and source are unknown, produce an entirely different protein, or a substance called RNA which is not a protein at all, the workings of which are not clear. A gene sometimes tosses ingredients (exons) into stuff being put out by entirely different genes, even distant genes in different chromosomes. It also turns out that other molecules associated with the DNA but not previously thought to have anything to do with it are responsible for inherited traits.

How Dry We Are.
After 2010, the accelerating depredations of fossil-fuel-intensive, chemical-saturated, genetically mutilated farming

practices were exacerbated, and in some ways obscured, by intensifying and spreading drought. It began in south Texas in 2010 and had spread by early 2013 to 80% of the contiguous United States. The drastically reduced harvest, in what had been forecast to be a bumper-crop year, was an earthquake that raised a tsunami of price increases that rolled through first the commodities markets and then the food markets.

According to researchers from the New England Complex Systems Institute, commodity speculation — bets placed by hedge funds and investment banks — wildly amplified clues and predictions about the future state of the markets. Using models that included the effects of speculation (whose very existence is strenuously denied by financiers and industrial ag tycoons) the Institute saw the threat of "global catastrophe driven by a speculator amplified food price bubble."

In the United States, where the average consumer spends well under 10 per cent of her income on food, predictions of a 15-cent increase in the price of a loaf of bread did not raise much alarm. For hundreds of thousands of people around the world, however, another spike in food prices constituted a death sentence. And the notion that only their end of the boat is sinking is bogus.

The more unstable the world, the more failed states and refugees, the more wars for resources, the more dangerous life becomes for us all. During the Arab Spring of early 2011, a dozen countries were wracked by civil unrest in the wake of a global spike in food prices.

It's Not the Heat, It's the Toxicity

Even in severe drought, when corn is unable to form kernels, it is still a big, edible plant. As Illinois rancher Steve Foglesong told the *Wall Street Journal* in 2012, "It may not have any ears on it, but it makes pretty good cow feed." Maybe not. Thirsty corn plants don't assimilate synthetic fertilizer well, and their lower leaves tend to accumulate concentrations of nitrates that can kill cows. Reuters reported that panicked feeders were overwhelming testing labs in the Midwest in the summer of 2012 trying to find out if the corn stalks they had left could safely be used as feed.

Meanwhile, down at the roots of the corn plants, tendrils reaching out desperately in search of water were being cut off by rootworms. This was remarkable, because most of the corn planted in the US is Monsanto genetically mutilated corn, engineered to be toxic to rootworms. Turned out it was only toxic to *some* rootworms. The rest were feasting on the (expensive) corn and multiplying happily, especially in Minnesota and Illinois. Turns out the only thing they like better than rootworm-resistant corn is dry weather.

Monsanto's other major gifts to industrial agriculture — Roundup and Roundup-Ready crops — continued their transformation into gifts that keep on taking. Roundup resistant weeds, especially pigweed, flourished in America's drought-stunted, worm-eaten crops. Resistant pigweed in 2012 infected at least half the cotton fields of the South, according to the *Southeast Farm Press*. Desperate farmers in several states, those who had any hope of a harvest at all, were hiring laborers to weed their fields by hand.

Back to the Future

It is supposed to be a Chinese proverb that humankind, for all its accomplishments and pretensions, depends for its existence on a six-inch layer of topsoil and frequent rain. We have in our industrial hysteria of the past hundred years killed our topsoil, poisoned the rain, and now, having laid hands on the tree of life itself, are in the process of corrupting the very seeds of our existence.

I return ever more infrequently to the farm where I grew up. Some years ago I stood on the porch of the empty and moldering house – my parents are long dead, the land is leased –

and looked out over the twilight prairie. Where yard- and house-lights used to twinkle, looking like ships in busy commerce on some great sea, there is now only darkness, all the people and most of the farm buildings are gone. Five miles away where our town was -- the general store, the hardware store, the feed store, two gas stations, the co-op, the post office, five elevators, the train station, the barber shop, the Chinese restaurant, the lumber yard, the church, the schools, the rink and a dozen or more homes -- exactly two buildings remain, the rink and the general store, empty and rotting.

From the dead porch I was surveying the dead soil of what had been one of the most fertile and inexhaustible regions on the planet, and it had been depopulated as if by war or famine or drought. Not by the failure of the soil, not yet, the relentless applications of chemicals still drag crops from the zombie earth. But industrialization has required the enlargement of the farm units from an average of a section (640 acres) or two in my grandfather's time to the five or ten thousand acres required for profitability by his grandchildren.

The thought that crossed my mind then, in that gathering darkness, was how ironic it was that one of the consequences of industrial agriculture was depopulation.

Chapter Two: The Fat of the Land

The condition of industrial agriculture would be dire enough if we ate what we grew, but the situation is at least an order of magnitude worse because we Americans eat so much meat -- 220 pounds per year for every one of us. The implications of that number are dismaying for anyone interested in sustainability. The way the industrialists do it, it takes 4.5 pounds of grain to produce a pound of edible chicken, over seven pounds for a pound of pork and a full 20 pounds of grain for a pound of beef. Fully 90 per cent of the grain consumed by Americans is in the form of meat and dairy products.

As with other wretched excesses of our consumption habits, such as big cars and extravagant houses, our diet has become a gold standard for the world; the workers of China and India and the rest of the developing world measure their emergence from poverty by the amount of meat they can afford to eat. In India, for example, per capita meat consumption averages just 12 pounds per year. If the world's poor get their wish, and begin to eat

220 pounds of meat a year just like Americans, all the grain the world can produce would be enough to feed fewer than 4 of every 10 people now alive.[19]

Or think of it another way. At the beginning of the process that brought those two eight-ounce steaks to your table -- at the very beginning -- some industrial farmer squandered 140 pounds of topsoil. And that was just the beginning.

Tastes Kinda Like Chicken

When the owner of the little chicken-processing plant in New Market, Virginia asked if I wanted to see the killing line, I didn't hesitate to say yes. Decades earlier, as a 12-year-old kid growing up on our farm, I often had the duty of decapitating, gutting and plucking the chicken that would a few hours later grace our Sunday dinner table. City dwellers, and others who get all their food wrapped in plastic, will gather from that information that I was not a squeamish kid, but might not understand that neither was I a callous kid. Living with the animals you use for food does not mean that you do not care for them, even love them, while they are with you. I have been inordinately fond of certain chickens in my life, especially Lucy, who loved to have her back scratched, sometimes joined me on the tractor as I went about farm business, and repeatedly tried to sneak into the house -- I think she thought she should live there.

My two oldest children learned about the duality of caring for animals and then using them for food when my daughter Kim was three years old and my son Jason was seven. Our milk cow gave birth to a calf, and I told them sternly that as we planned to raise this calf for food, we would not be giving it a name. Within hours it had somehow acquired the name "Ferdinand." When, six months or so later, it came time for the calf to be sent to the butcher's, everyone was told what was going on, just another day

19 Roberts, Paul *The End of Food.* New York: Houghton Mifflin Co. 2008 p. 211

on the farm, no need for dramatics. Everyone did well until the cattle truck was pulling out of the yard, when as its sound faded away we heard a sweet, three-year-old voice saying plaintively, "Good-bye, Ferdinand." Everybody cried. A few weeks later we sat down at our table to dig into a juicy meat loaf. Suddenly, Jason stopped, his laden fork halfway to his mouth. He looked at me. "Is this Ferdinand?" he asked. Bent on honesty, I looked steadily back at him. "Yes," I said. "Hm," he replied, chewing, "Pretty good."

So when I went around the corner of the chicken-processing plant to where the trucks were backed in with their crates of squawking birds, then through the door to the bay where men were grabbing the chickens and hanging them upside down, by their feet, on the overhead conveyor, I was not at all prepared for the impact of what I was about to see.

The chickens quieted as the line moved steadily forward. Two guide rails forming a long V closed against their necks until there was just room for them to pass. Then they came to what looked like a bicycle tire, turning horizontally as the chickens paraded by. Below the bicycle-tire apparatus extended another circle, of razor-sharp steel, that neatly and without effort severed each passing chicken head from its neck. The heads dropped -- plop, plop, plop, plop, all day and all night long -- into a conveyor that carried them away. The blood ran into a gurgling drain that carried it off. The convulsing bodies sailed on toward plucking, evisceration, cooling and packaging.

I have rarely experienced such horror as I did at that sight. It made me think of the films I had seen of the Nazi death camps of World War II. There is something about industrial-scale killing, even of animals, even to someone used to hog-butchering and deer-gutting and poultry-plucking, that is unspeakably awful. Just seeing it, let alone participating in it, you feel your soul corrode.

Nor is this revulsion a matter of mere aesthetics. Deer hunters know that the quality of their venison is directly related to the quality of the kill. Wound the animal, chase it for hours, and your meat will be tainted with adrenaline -- the bitter residue of terror and agony. Take him unawares with a clean shot and enjoy the sweetness of a life well lived and well ended.

What, then, shall we expect of the nightmarish world in which our meat animals live and die?

The Double Breasted Six Week Superchicken

The chickens that are hung on the killing line these days are six weeks old. Had they lived to be seven weeks old, their legs probably would have begun to break down under the freakish weight of their enlarged chest, the result of relentless genetic manipulation to give the consumer more of what she wants, which is white meat. (Actually, it happens to roughly one in four broilers before they're old enough to butcher.[20]) Had they not been crippled by their ungainly bodies, or by the inability of their comparatively stunted hearts and lungs to supply oxygen to their tissues, they would have begun to sicken from having been virtually force-fed corn, which their digestive systems are not equipped to handle, and overdosed on antibiotics whose purpose is to keep them alive -- despite their hot, dirty, crowded quarters, alien food, grotesque physique and stunted immune response -- long enough to slaughter.

Those chickens that make it to the killing line are beheaded (at the rate of 70 per minute), drained, and then torn open by machines that can eviscerate them faster than an undocumented immigrant. But the machines often rupture the intestines as they tear them out, drenching the carcass with their contents, including chicken shit. All right, make that fecal matter. The rubber fingers of the plucking machines spread the slime from bird to bird, after which the carcasses are cooled in a huge vat of cold water, which in short order becomes a fecal soup. Gerald Kuester of the US Department of Agriculture has been quoted as saying, "At the end

---

20 Roberts, p. 76

of the line, the birds are no cleaner than if they had been dipped in a toilet." Make that an un-flushed toilet.[21]

According to the Physicians Committee for Responsible Medicine, a non-profit organization of about 5,000 physicians and 100,000 supporting members, up to 15% of the weight of industrial chicken on sale in this country is fecal soup. In 2006, the group filed a petition with the US Department of Agriculture to warn the public about the health hazards posed by American poultry, and to urge the government clean up. Still waiting.

The chicken industry is worried about the quality of its meat, but not because it contains fecal matter (they continue to resist successfully all efforts to require the USDA to label shit found in food a contaminant, let alone to label industrial chicken, as the Physicians Committee recommended, a bio-hazard). What does concern them is a condition known to insiders as PSE -- pale, soft, exudative meat. The genetic manipulations that produce those huge chicken breasts so swiftly do not provide the muscle with an adequate blood supply -- some of the tissue in a living bird sometimes actually dies. In addition, the six-week life cycle does not give the muscle time to form fully, with the result that the meat tends to be, to use the term of art, "inelastic." Moreover, on execution, the breast muscle -- which is fast-twitch tissue capable of the rapid contractions necessary for winged flight (Remember? They are *birds!*) -- convulse and discharge excess lactic acid into the meat. As Paul Roberts writes in *The End of Food,* "The acids denature the proteins in the meat, which causes the meat to turn pale, lose its ability to retain moisture (hence the bloody residue at the bottom of the package in the grocery store), and become so soft that it crumbles when cooked."

The oblivious consumer, noting only that chicken is cheap (less than one-quarter its 1980 cost, adjusted for inflation) has tripled his intake of the stuff, to nearly 40 billion pounds a year,

---

21 Posting on Care2.com: http://www.care2.com/c2c/share/detail/127259

nearly 90 pounds for each one of us. 22

Corned Beef

The lives and deaths of the cattle that provide steaks for our four-star restaurants and burgers for our fast-food places are scarcely better than those of industrial chickens. Cattle have not been as disfigured by genetic manipulation, although tinkering has raised their typical slaughter weight by about 300 pounds. For six months, nearly half their lifespan, cattle live a relatively normal life, grazing open fields among their kin. For this activity -- grazing -- cattle are wonderfully adapted. Unlike most creatures, they possess a rumen, in which the grass they ingest is fermented, in fact digested for them, by colonies of bacteria. Left to its own devices, a cow settles into its grassy ecosystem, fertilizing the pasture on which it grazes, and in four or five years will have converted roughage we humans cannot digest into a thousand pounds or so of the protein we love.23

Not nearly fast enough for industry. So at the age of six months, cattle are wrenched from their mothers (to the protracted distress of both animals, sometimes leading to sickness) and confined in what is euphemistically called a "backgrounding" pen, where they learn to live in close confinement, and to eat corn from a trough. After two months in this purgatory, they go to cow hell.

The cattle will spend the rest of their lives standing ankle deep in their own manure, crowded and jostled continuously, in front of bunkers containing mostly corn, along with whatever other form of protein the feedlot operators can buy cheap and persuade the cows to ingest -- sugar beet waste, potato scraps, cottonseed meal, chicken litter, anything that is dense in calories. (Until 1997 their diet often included cow parts left over from slaughterhouses, but then that form of cannibalism was identified as the source -- the only source -- of the spread of mad cow disease. Thereafter the

22 Roberts, *End of Food* p. 71-5
23 Pollan, *Omnivore's Dillemma* p. 71

FDA banned the practice -- *except for blood products and fat*.) The object is to make the cattle fat, of course, and not just with fatty deposits but with streaks of fat throughout the muscle tissue. It's called marbling, in a steak, or juicy, in a hamburger, and consumers demand it. They seem not to care that the fat of corn-fed cattle contains much less of the beneficial omega-3 fatty acids and much more undesirable saturated fat than that of grass-fed animals.

But the problem for the industry is not the quality of the fat; it's the fact that the cows' diet makes them sick. They bloat, because the excess starch and the lack of roughage in the corn forms a slime that traps the gas generated by fermentation in the rumen and, untreated, can suffocate the animal. The corn also changes the pH in the rumen from neutral, which is normal in cows, to highly acidic, which leads to heartburn -- acidosis -- so severe it can kill. These afflictions, being chronic in the feedlot, lead to others -- liver disease, ulcers, diarrhea -- and to a depression of the immune system that opens the door to even more serious diseases and infections such as pneumonia, coccidiosis, even a form of polio. It is fortunate for the producers that the cattle are ready for slaughter in five months because they could not survive the feed lot much longer. As with the chickens, the only reason they do live long enough to be killed is that they are typically dosed heavily and constantly with antibiotics.[24]

This Little Pig Got Sick

When the industrialization of chickens cut into the market for pork, pigs got industrialized. In the twenty years after 1980, the number of hog lots declined by more than 90 per cent, from over half a million to less than half a thousand, while the average number of hogs per lot increased more than tenfold, to over a thousand. [25]

---

24 Pollan, *Omnivore's Dilemma* pps. 75-8
25   Roberts p. 72

Let's not call them pig farms, as the industry likes to do because it calls up images of grandpa's red barn, bucolic fields, bright mornings, Babe, and Charlotte's Web. Hog lots are grim, enormous gulags comprised of vast expanses of bare concrete floors and steel cages. These factories consume enormous amounts of energy, needed to deliver food and water, to maintain optimum temperature (not for the comfort of the animals, but so that they don't waste energy trying to keep warm or cool down instead of growing meat) and to dispose of amounts of sewage typical of a small town. When a sow has a litter (the industry average is 20 piglets), she is confined in a farrowing crate that prevents her from interrupting nursing by turning around or getting up, so that soreness and infection of her teats is constant. When the piglets are a few weeks old they are weaned and jammed into concrete-and-steel cells to await their conversion to bacon.

As they wait, there are only two things to do – eat and defecate. Naturally inquisitive and playful animals, the intelligence of pigs is rated above that of the average dog, about that of a three-year-old child. Deprived of all comfort, freedom, diversion and activity, they go mad. They would bite each other's tails, but at weaning their tails are docked and their teeth pulled (males are castrated), all without anesthetic, which is not cost-effective.

For decades, as long as these methods endangered only pigs, they failed to arouse the opposition of any but the most dedicated animal-rights activists. Recently, however, real and present dangers to humans have emerged from human treatment of pigs.

One of the most problematic arises out of the fact that close confinement of large numbers of any animal subjects them to communicable disease and infections. To forestall this, pigs are heavily dosed with antibiotics, not to treat illness but to prevent it. The result among pigs, as among humans, is that the antibiotics kill most but not all of the infectious bacteria; the surviving, resistant bacteria replicate, and you're back where you started, without an effective medicine. These superbugs, more staidly referred to as

MRSA (methicillin-resistant Staphylococcus aureus, pronounced "mersa") started emerging in our hospitals in the 1990s and ten years thereafter in our hog lots. According to the New York Times, MRSA kills more Americans every year – 18,000 – than does the AIDS epidemic. [26]

It is well established that hog lots in the Netherlands and Canada are breeding grounds for MRSA. In the one study done thus far in the United States, in 2009, the superbug was found in 49 per cent of the pigs and 45 per cent of the workers in two hog operations in Iowa and Illinois.[27]

Sick and Sicker

The conditions in which turkeys, milk cows and laying hens are kept by industrial agriculture are similarly abusive. But the main point here is not to recruit you into the ranks of vegans, or People for the Ethical Treatment of Animals. However unkind, or even fatal to the animals, these methods are, the real danger is to us, on whose behalf they are thus treated. When the proverbial canary in the coal mine drops dead in his cage for lack of air, we do not try to revive him, protest his treatment, or sign petitions to keep canaries out of coal mines; *we get our asses out of the coal mine before we die, too.*

One quarter of all Americans are affected by food-borne toxins and infections each year; about 325,000 have to go to a hospital, and more than 5,000 die. It has always been the case, of course, that food is subject to contamination by pathogens. Typically these have included salmonella, long the most common source of food-borne illness (nearly half of cases in 2004), one strain of which causes typhoid fever. (In the summer of 2008, 1442 people in 43 states, the District of Columbia and Canada were sickened by salmonella contaminating jalapeño and Serrano

---

26 Kristof, Nicholas. "Pathogens in Our Pork," *The New York Times,* 03/14/09.

27   Smith TC, Male MJ, Harper AL, Kroeger JS, Tinkler GP, et al. (2009) "Methicillin-Resistant *Staphylococcus aureus* (MRSA) Strain ST398 Is Present in Midwestern US Swine and Swine Workers."

peppers.) Less obtrusive but long with us is listeria, a microbe that rarely infects humans but has a vicious mortality rate of 25%. 28

During the past 20 years or so the threat of food-borne illness has intensified because of so-called emergent pathogens, microbes whose nature and behavior have changed dramatically, often because of the practices of industrial agriculture. Just the close confinement of large numbers of animals or birds, a prerequisite of industrial-agriculture profitability, ensures the spread of microbes and maximizes their opportunities for changing their behavior in response to new conditions. For example, in the 1980s, *salmonella enteritidis* somehow made its way into chicken embryos and began to spread by way of eggs without sickening its host chicken.29 Today, *campylobacter* (the second most common source of food borne illness) infects virtually all the raw chicken meat on the market.

Perhaps the most ominous threat to public health, and the most ominous indictment of industrial agriculture practices, is offered by the progress of *Escherichia coli* bacteria. Hundreds of strains of *E. coli* are and always have been ubiquitous in the guts of ruminants -- which is to say grass-eating animals. In general, the bacteria are harmless to humans, primarily because the contents of a ruminant's digestive tract are neither acidic nor alkaline, while the stomach contents of a human are acidic enough to kill the bacteria. Or they used to be.

That changed in the 1980s. The sugar in corn, as we have seen, acidifies a cow's stomach, with effects not only on the cow. At first the acidity kills most, but not all, *E. coli* bacteria; but the survivors pass on their accidental resistance, and at length the cow's gut is repopulated with bacteria tough enough to live happily in a human. Worse, around the same time, *E. coli* struck up a partnership with another microbe, *shigella*, from which it acquired

---

28 USDA Food Safety and Inspection Service, Centers for Disease Control and Prevention.
29 Roberts p. 180

the ability to produce a set of virulent toxins known as shiga toxins. One of the *E. coli* strains thus equipped, $O_{157}:H_7$, does not affect cattle, but in humans can perforate intestinal walls, infect the blood and destroy the kidneys. It is so potent that this can be accomplished by the ingestion of just 50 bacteria.

Today, *E. coli* is found in half of all feedlot cattle – in the summertime, 80% of them. It is spread to vegetable crops by the feces of carrier animals, by floodwaters and runoff tainted with manure, even by dust in the wind, to which the tenacious E coli can cling even after a protracted drought. Whether on the carcasses of animals or on leaves of spinach (which spread a disastrous outbreak in 2006), it shrugs off refrigeration and chlorine rinses.[30]

The meat industry has shrugged off efforts to label, let alone eliminate, the contaminants in its food with a combination of campaign donations [*see Chapter Five: The Failed State*] and the argument that its products are perfectly safe as long as the consumer cooks them properly, that is, heats the meat to a temperature high enough to kill the bacteria. Although no water department in the world could get away with delivering water that is safe *as long as you boil it and filter it before drinking it,* the food industry has enjoyed remarkable success in avoiding responsibility for the safety of what they sell. In 1992, after *E. coli* sickened 600 people, most of them children, and killed four (because a burger chain undercooked its meat to keep it "juicy") the USDA finally classified *E. coli* as an adulterant, but other pathogens remain under a don't-ask-don't-tell policy.

Shoot the Messenger
In the summer of 2011, the US Department of Agriculture received a report it had commissioned on the rise of infectious bacteria that are resistant to antibiotics. The report — not a study, but a survey of existing studies — warned of a "growing public health concern worldwide" as more and more people are sickened and killed by

---

30 Roberts pp 182-3, 193

infections against which modern medicines are helpless. (Just one of them, MRSA, now kills more people every year than AIDS.) And it was a powerful indictment of industrial agriculture's role in creating these so-called "superbugs." So the USDA did just what you would expect the government regulator of industrial agriculture to do: it buried the report.

The USDA first posted the report on its website, pointing out that the studies referenced in the report were all from "reputed, scientific, peer-reviewed and scholarly journals." Obviously, that was written by a low-level staffer who was not in touch with the big picture, and who still believed in "science." But before we review the short life and nasty end of the report, let's review what was in it.

The report summarized 63 scholarly papers that looked at the effects of administering large quantities of antibiotics to animals being raised for food in confined, crowded, stressful conditions with unnatural diets. The antibiotics are given not to make sick animals well, but to keep all the animals well enough to put on weight — that means profit — and make it to slaughter. It is pretty well known now that the practice kills off bacteria that are not naturally resistant to the antibiotic, while those that survive, thrive, and soon the whole population consists of superbugs that, when they infect humans, cannot be killed.

Just in outline, that sounds bad. But this report got more specific about how bad:

> "Antimicrobial-resistant strains of foodborne pathogens are widespread throughout the world. Most of these resistant pathogens ... acquire their resistance in food animal host before they transmit and infect human beings via the consumption of contaminated food. Therefore, foods of animal origin are frequently associated with antimicrobial-resistant foodborne disease outbreaks. Some foods that have been associated with antimicrobial-resistant infections and outbreaks include: chicken, beef, pork, dairy products

70

and salad vegetables.

"The increasing rate of [antibiotic resistance] has raised the concern that we may enter the 'post antibiotic era' where no effective antibiotics for treating several life-threatening infections would be available."

Days after it appeared on the USDA website, and in a matter-of-fact report on the *Dow Jones Newswires*, the industry cleared its throat. The chief veterinarian of the National Pork Producers Council, Liz Wagstrom, opined (for the journal *National Hog Farmer*): "We find it very disappointing that a research assistant at a university, who is not an Agricultural Research Service scientist can develop and post such a review without it going through an agency or peer review process."

Wait a minute. Only an Agricultural Research Service scientist can report what scientists all over the world are finding? And why does a report that quotes only peer-reviewed studies have to be peer reviewed? Never mind, you could almost hear the yelp from USDA at the touch of the lash. And you could see it, in the form of a new disclaimer that appeared in bright red over the study on the website: "This technical review was written by a university cooperator. This review has not been peer reviewed. The views expressed in this publication do not necessarily reflect the views of the United States Department of Agriculture."

A few weeks later, the report vanished altogether. And the USDA ordered the researcher who wrote it never to speak to the news media about it.

I Feel Fluish

Although it has not yet been realized, by far the worst potential threat to public health from food animals is that of flu. There are three basic strains of influenza – swine, avian and human – and pigs get them all. Since pigs typically live their lives in close confinement with thousands of other pigs, whatever flu they get spreads rapidly, and in the manner of viruses, mutates frequently.

Whatever new kind of flu is thus created, the pigs readily give to their human handlers.

The avian influenza virus is universally present in wild birds, but does not affect them. Spread by their feces and bodily fluids, it is very contagious among birds, and easily jumps from migratory to domestic ducks and geese, who usually are sickened but not quickly killed, and thus have time to intermingle with and infect chickens. Among domesticated chickens bird flu can turn lethal, killing more than 90% of a flock within 48 hours. In 1997, the virus suddenly developed the ability to attack humans -- six people died in an outbreak in Hong Kong.

Since then three subtypes of avian flu have developed an ability to infect humans who come in contact with sick birds. Of these the most dangerous is H_5N_1. Its incidence in humans is relatively rare -- the World Health Organization reported 38 cases, most of them in Indonesia, during 2008. The good news is that in almost every case, the flu spread from bird to human, and was unable to spread from human to human. More ominously, 29 of those people died. Public officials around the world live in a state of fear that this highly adaptable virus is going to mutate -- possibly by infecting a person carrying a human influenza -- to a form easily communicable from human to human. If that happens, migratory birds and globe-trotting humans will spread the disease rapidly around the world.[31] The last time that happened, in 1918-19, between 30 and 50 million people, including 675,000 Americans, died.[32]

The world got a bad scare in the spring of 2009, when a strain of flu suddenly appeared in Mexico that at first appeared to contain attributes of all three strains of flu (although it was mistakenly labeled "swine flu") and was highly communicable from human to human. According to the federal Centers for

---

[31] Centers for Disease Control: www.cdc.gov/flu/avian/outbreaks/current.htm;_
[32] US Department of Health and Human Services: http://1918.pandemicflu. gov/the_pandemic/index.htm

Disease Control and the World Health Organization, within two months 15,000 people had been infected in 48 countries, and nearly a hundred had died. For a couple of weeks, it was widely feared that the onslaught of H1N1 flu was the long-feared global pandemic, but it proved, at least in its first outing, to be no worse than the garden-variety, seasonal flu that we have all learned to live with.

On the Road Again

Of all the industrial practices that threaten to reduce or interrupt our supply of food -- soil destruction, pollution, chemical overdosing, petroleum addiction, genetic mutilation, monoculture vulnerability, diversity reduction and so on -- the most deadly, most imminent and least discussed may be the best-management practice referred to as "Just-in-time" inventory control.

Articulated by Henry Ford, pioneered by the Southern grocery chain Piggly Wiggly, made famous by Toyota (they adopted it in 1938, having learned it from Piggly Wiggly) and unleashed by Internet communications in the 1990s, Just-in-time supply eliminates warehousing and a large percentage of inventory. It uses the immediacy of computerized inventory control and world-wide communications to order supplies only when they are about to be needed, with delivery timed to be effected exactly when they are needed.

The grocery business has universally adopted Just-in-time, with the result that an individual store contains enough food to meet demand for perhaps three days. Anything beyond that depends on the timely arrival at the store's loading dock of 18-wheeler trucks, referred to by Wal-Mart managers as their "rolling warehouses." This is not just a matter of carting lettuce from California to New York, beef from the slaughterhouses of Illinois to Florida, or chicken from the mid-Atlantic states to Oregon; many of those trucks cannot depart their loading docks until the arrival of cargo aircraft from all over the world. About 25,000 shipments of food arrive in the US every day from more than 100

73

countries, into which agriculture has been pushed in search of more cheap land and labor, as well as fewer regulations on the treatment of the environment and the population. Anchovies come from Thailand, dry apricots from Turkey, grapes from Chile, sesame seeds from India, sweet cured plums from China. At the border checkpoint near Nogales, Mexico, in the peak winter season, almost 1,000 produce trucks arrive daily, carrying eggplants, cucumbers, tomatoes, peppers and other products. According to government agencies, imports account for 80% of the nation's seafood, 45% of its fresh fruit and 17% of its fresh vegetables. 33

All of this works well when it works. But in moving all food reserves into the transportation net, and extending that net around the world, the food industry has not only maximized its profits, it has maximized the risk that any interruption in the supply chain will be catastrophic.

The most likely trigger would be a sudden decrease in the supply of petroleum, or increase in its cost, as a result of terrorist attack, foreign embargo, natural disaster, oilfield exhaustion or other event. For example, a Katrina-like hurricane (the number and intensity of which are increasing because of global climate change) that more directly hits the Gulf of Mexico oil-drilling platforms, the Gulf Coast oil refining industry, or shuts down the Port of New Orleans, would have serious food-supply consequences.

Another possibility is the inevitable massive earthquake that is expected to inflict the worst natural disaster in US history on the Los Angeles-San Diego-Baja California region. The distribution of food, petroleum and all other commodities from the Pacific Ocean to the Mississippi River will be catastrophically disrupted.

---

33 *USA Today*, "US Food Imports Outrun FDA Resources" 03/18/2007:
Energy Bulletin, "Is Just-in-Time Nearly Out of Time?" *www.energybulletin.net*

The Fat of the Land

These, then, are the sources of our food; vast expanses of dead and toxic dirt, enormous warehouses of sick and suffering animals. From the fields come great mechanized rivers of grain, most of it for feeding to the sick animals, the rest to be fashioned by food engineers into Twinkies and Cheesies and Sugar Pops. From the slaughter houses come bins and slabs of flaccid meat injected with various embalming fluids devised by food engineers to hold it together and make it look natural and fresh until its expiration date. This is how we get our food, just in time, from a vast fleet of cargo jets and 18-wheelers roaring through the night, drawing on a fuel lifeline that runs all the way to Arabia and is starting to suck air. This is how we have become a nation of obese, malnourished people about to be disconnected from our feeding tube.

Against this great killing tide some powerful and refreshing streams are running. The sustainable agriculture movement, led by people such as Joel Salatin of Virginia, is rediscovering the power of diversity and the joy of farming with, instead of against, nature. To visit his farm, as I did a decade ago, is to see ground that is vibrant with life, that instead of being exhausted by the bounty taken from it each year – eggs, chicken, turkey, rabbit, pork, beef – actually increases in volume, quality and fertility. The organic gardening movement, pioneered by J.I. Rodale in 1942, is dedicated to cleansing our food of the poisons used to make it more profitable. While its methods and mindset are essential to the production of wholesome food, they have been co-opted by industrial agriculture, and by the time profits have been maximized with large-scale monoculture and petroleum-intensive growing, harvesting and transportation, the advantages gained by reduced chemical use seem dismayingly small. Yet more and more people are coming together in various ways -- the slow food movement, the local food movement -- to try to reclaim nutritious food and a sustainable way of life from the jaws of industrial agriculture.

Fresh water runs into the ocean from all the rivers, and yet the salty ocean does not change its nature. Human nature does not change much either, and when we are presented with a choice between doing good and doing harm, when the good thing is expensive and difficult and the harmful thing is cheap and easy, we will almost always go with the cheap and easy. The money does not change. Those who accumulate a great deal of it will spend it freely to maintain the conditions that made their wealth possible. They will scream tyranny if asked to pay taxes to maintain the country that makes their existence possible, but cheerfully spend millions upon millions on advertising and on politicians to make sure that the millions keep on coming. Sustainable agriculture has no such cash resources, nor does diversity or the web of life. The future of the human race may depend upon them, but if they have no 30-second spots on *American Idol,* who's to know or care?

If this ocean is a dead zone, and all the rivers running into it cannot change it, then are the industrialists right to scorn the advocates of the methods of sustainable living? Are they right to say that chemical-free, diversified, small-scale farming can never feed the world's people? Yes they are, absolutely. But what they don't say and won't admit and find unthinkable is the undeniable fact that in a very short time, they will be unable to feed the world's people, either.

But while neither industrial agriculture nor sustainable agriculture can feed the world as it now is, let alone sustain present rates of growth, yet we need not despair. Because sustainable farming can sustain you and your family, and me and my family, long after petro-chemical-industrial food is a distant, unpleasant memory.

PART II. WATER

"Whiskey is for drinking; water is for fighting over"

Mark Twain (attributed)

Chapter Three: A Drinking Problem

From the window of the airliner approaching Atlanta's international airport in the summer of 2007, Lake Lanier was a stunning sight. With its 38,000 acres of sparkling blue water and its 700 miles of serpentine shore, it was always impressive. But what dropped my jaw that day was the immense, bathtub-ring stain of brown mud flats, hundreds of feet wide, between the vegetation marking the normal shoreline and the present edge of the water. The bleak expanse was studded with forlorn stretches of stranded docks, piers and swimming platforms, sitting high and dry on hard ground.

Lake Lanier is man-made (as are most lakes in the southern US), sprawling behind a dam erected in 1956 on the Chattahoochee River about 35 miles northwest of, and upstream from, Atlanta. It was built to protect the city from floods, and to provide it with hydroelectric power. But in the ensuing four decades the population of the metro area tripled – it was 1.5 million in 1960 and passed five million in 2004. In the 1990s, Atlanta was among the fastest-growing cities in the world, adding a million new inhabitants every ten years after 1990, and early in the new millennium became the fastest-growing city in the United States. This growth occurred despite the fact that Atlanta is located nowhere near a major river or other source of water. Unlike most other major centers of commerce and population, the city did not begin as a port, but as a railroad town. And the fuse leading to its explosive growth was the building of its international airport in the 1950s. Largely because of its role as a communications hub, Atlanta is home base to more international corporations than any other American city except New York and Houston.

The only reason that Atlanta was able to grow without restraint was Lake Lanier. And in 2007, with the growth continuing unabated, Lake Lanier was giving out. Not long after I viewed it from the air it reached an all-time record low water level, more than 20 feet below normal. The entire Atlanta metro area was put on notice that it was *within 90 days of running out of water*. Carol Couch, the director of the Environmental Protection Division in Georgia, told ABC News, "Without any intervention, we are likely to run out of water in three months."

Imagine five million people without water. It would be a disaster of Biblical proportions that would bring the region, if not the entire country, to its knees. The city responded by restricting the watering of lawns. It asked whether businesses in Atlanta would mind doing their best to reduce water use by 10%. But its counties continued to ignore a water conservation plan devised in 2003 by the Metropolitan North Georgia Water Planning District that involved fixing leaks and charging more for high water consumption. The only thing that Atlanta insisted on, 90 days from disaster, was less watering of lawns.

Lawn Order

Let's just take a moment to consider the lawn. If another culture ever does an anthropological study of our folkways, it will have to conclude that to us, lawns were religious icons. As with cathedrals, Christmas light displays, and various forms of ecclesiastical costume, only religious zeal can explain the amount of time and money that lawnists spend on their displays. As with cathedrals, the object of the lawn is to instill awe, and penny pinching is no way to get there; lawnists pay almost as much per square foot to lay sod on their front yards as to carpet their living rooms. As with the robes of cardinals, the lawn is there to be admired, not to do anything so prosaic as to provide food or shelter. As with Amish dress the simplicity -- the exclusion of everything but simple grass -- is rigorous. And as with the Arab burqa, everything must be covered, no exceptions, with the same color.

Lawnists drench their patches of grass with fertilizers and pesticides at concentrations and application rates higher than those seen on any farm, with the excess gurgling away through storm sewers to poison the nearest river. Lawnists buy enormous riding tractors with which to mow their little patch, and a noisy leaf blower with which to blast any errant leaf into the street or their neighbor's yard. They drench their lawns with water it as if the grass were rice growing in a paddy. Like most religionists, they constantly compare their blessings with those of their neighbors. And if you want a glimpse of fundamentalist extremist rage, let an errant child or dog soil a lawnist's shrine. All this so that their eyes can occasionally alight upon the object of their devotion and find it to be a more perfect expanse of empty green than their neighbors'. (All those lawn-care commercials featuring happy families at play on their grass? Forget them. For one thing the chemical concentrations found on the typical lawn could kill a mastodon. For another, playing might hurt the grass.)

So it was perhaps not trivial that Atlanta reacted to the threat of running out of water -- in 90 days! -- not with restraints on building and development, not with requirements for efficient plumbing, but with restrictions on watering lawns. Any suggestion that there might be a limit to the number of people who could drink from the same lake drew ferocious response from the people who developed real estate, built houses and funded campaigns for public office. "People are coming to this state whether environmentalists like it or not," said Ed Phillips of the Georgia Home Builders Association. "What are we going to do? Put up a fence?"

Consider the structure of this argument, because it is generic. Mr. Phillips first invoked the freedom of the people to do what they wish to do without restriction -- ignoring the fact that most people move to a place like Atlanta in response to lavish advertising campaigns by chambers of commerce and real-estate developers. He then attributed any and all objections to suicidal growth to "environmentalists," who of course are assumed to be a small, radical, special-interest group. Then he defined false alternatives: either proceed without change or build a wall. Although devoid of content and logic, the argument was backed by enough cash to make it persuasive to Atlanta politicians, who began to clamor for the building of more reservoirs.

The industrialists and their politicians labored to place on someone else he blame for any inconvenience that might be caused by lack of water. They said the US Army Corps of Engineers, who built and cared for the dam and Lake Lanier, was at fault for mistakenly releasing downstream more water than they should have, because a malfunctioning meter had told them that the lake level was higher than it really was. They said the two-year drought in the region (and by extension, global warming) was at fault for reducing water supplies, never mind the orders-of-magnitude increases on the demand side. They said the states downstream, who also seemed to feel they had rights to the Chattahoochee River, were at fault for claiming too much water from "Atlanta's" lake; Florida to preserve a species of mussel in Apalachicola Bay ("It's a choice between humans and mussels," blared outraged

Atlantans), and Alabama to cool a downstream power plant that keeps the lights on for humans in Alabama, which of course represents a choice between them and Atlanta humans.

Just as lawn envy and living in denial were reaching intolerable levels in Atlanta, the city got the intervention it had been counting on. It rained, in the spring of 2008, the drought eased, and the whole crisis vanished from the public media and the public mind. For now.

What Happens in Vegas

There was no such respite for Las Vegas, a city of nearly two million people in the western desert between the Grand Canyon and Death Valley. Its only source of water is the Colorado River, which for the convenience of the seven states that depend on it has been dammed into a 110-mile long reservoir, Lake Mead, not far upstream from Vegas. Behind the storied Hoover Dam, Lake Mead is the largest such impoundment of water in the United States (although it is nearly matched by Lake Powell, not far upstream at the border of Utah and Arizona).

In the summer of 2008, because of steadily rising demand and a steadily worsening drought, Lake Mead was less than one-half full. Refilling the lake would take 20 years of "normal" flow of the Colorado River, and no climatologist expects ever again to see the Colorado flowing at a rate that was once considered normal. One of the consequences of the global climate change that is rapidly emerging from the theoretical into the actual is that the American West will receive much less rain in the future. When the Hoover Dam was built in the 1920s, the "normal" flow of the Colorado was estimated at 17.4 million acre-feet per year, an average that has seldom been achieved since, and that is nearly twice the recent average flow.[34]

At its present rate of depletion, the lake was expected to

---

34 Wood, Chris, *Dry Spring:The Coming Water Crisis of North America.* Raincoast Books, 2008 p. 144

drop below the Las Vegas intake as early as 2010, and no later than 2015. Like Atlanta, the city rejected calls for limits on its growth – it reached two million souls in 2008, having added about half a million since the turn of the millennium. Although the financial meltdown of 2008 crippled that growth rate, as well as the ability of governments to finance things like water projects, officials bristle at any suggestion that scarcity of water should interfere with their plans to get back on the fast track. Patricia Mulroy, manager of the Southern Nevada Water Authority, used this logic: "During the next 50 years, this country's population is expected to explode by another 140 million. Where do you want the people to go?"

To get ready for the people who are going to want to move to the desert to be near the casinos (with their fountains and water slides), the authority set crews to work excavating a 30-foot-wide shaft 600 feet straight down and three miles laterally, through solid rock. Their goal is to open a new water intake lower in the lake by 2012, which they hoped would be soon enough. For the longer term, they're planning pipelines to tap aquifers under the Utah border 327 miles away. 35 And there's wilder talk from city officials, about diverting the floodwaters of the Mississippi River or building a pipeline to the Great Lakes.36

The Drinking Problem

The basic facts about water are deceptively simple. There is plenty of it, and our individual need for it is modest. We live on the water planet, after all, so called because 70 per cent of its surface is covered by water. The amount of water present in the world does not change, has not varied since our home planet congealed from star dust and gathered around itself its thin, moist cloak of air. And all the water we humans need for survival is a modest 30 ounces --

35 Wood, *Dry Spring* p. 220
36 "Las Vegas Running Out of Water Means Dimming Los Angeles Lights" Bloomberg 02/26/2009

less than a liter -- per day (much of which is provided by the water content of the food we eat)..

On the other hand, most of the water on the planet is either salty or frozen, making it unavailable for drinking. Much of the rest is somewhere in the water cycle -- wafting along the wind as vapor, for example, or decorating a landscape as a cumulus cloud -- and likewise unavailable for slaking thirst. And while our individual need for water is not great, it is unrelenting. Our life expectancy without it is about three days in hot weather, perhaps ten days otherwise. That there is plenty of fresh water on the planet is scant comfort to someone stranded in the desert. Knowing that the average rainfall where you live is plentiful is of no help in the tenth year of a non-typical drought.

In nature, organisms that require water for their survival live near it, or in it. Frogs do not decide to trek into the desert to start a new frog colony dedicated to, let's say, gambling. Yes, there are Spadefoot Toads, which live in the desert, buried in a state of suspended animation for years until a freak rainstorm gives them the opportunity to emerge, breed and rebury themselves. They are mutants, caught by a changing climate, who adapted and evolved. Which is to say -- let us be clear -- that gazillions of normal toads died, leaving their hostile, new, arid world to the freaks. The engine of evolution is the death of the maladapted. Populations that wish to sustain themselves, as opposed to dying out to make way for early adapters to a new set of circumstances, have to enter into a relationship with their surroundings that is less dramatic than that of the Spadefoot Toad; generally they choose to live near water.

We humans, on the other hand, have got into the habit of changing the circumstances rather than adapting to them. Deprived of water, we indulge in water works. We began with wells that relieved us of the necessity of constant movement to keep up with the vagaries of the water cycle. Wells permitted more expansive and productive agriculture, which in turn allowed population growth, surpluses, trade and specialization, which led to cities. It is conceivable to abandon a farm if the rains do not come and a well runs dry, but a city? An imperial city? For the Romans and the Mayans, to cite just two examples, the next step was aqueducts. Now, not only did we not have to abandon our cities when water became scarce in a locality, but we could start a new city almost anywhere we wanted to live. Moreover, the corollaries of piped running water -- cleanliness of the supply and plumbing to deal with waste -- saved more lives than any public-health advance before or since. Thus there were soon more of us, living in more cities in more places.

Still, there were limits. There were practical limits to the diameter and length of aqueducts. While a closed aqueduct prevented contamination, the water was only as pure and abundant as its source, which could be affected by drought and pollution. Then there was the matter of the ever growing stream of waste flowing downhill to pollute the watershed below.

The true industrialization of water began in the United States by the second decade of the 20th Century. It involved the creation of enormous central treatment plants where water is filtered and disinfected by the application of chlorine. Keeping up with the demands of population growth, especially in urban centers, has required the construction of vast ingathering networks, to get raw water to the processing plants, and a similarly enormous distribution network.

The waste implicit in the industrialization of water is stupendous. For one thing the cost to consumers is kept artificially low by politicians who love to appear to be giving something for nothing. Americans typically pay between $1.25 and $3.00 for a thousand gallons of drinking water. In many cities, New York being one example, householders pay a flat fee for their water no matter how much they use. This bargain is made possible because municipalities are recovering from fees little more than their bare operating expenses, with little provision for maintenance and eventual replacement of the enormous infrastructure.37 Thus unrestrained by cost, nine of every ten Americans who draw their water from public water systems use about 80 gallons per day -- that's about 200 gallons per day per household.

Yet in another sense the expense of delivering industrialized water is unnecessarily high, because every drop is filtered and chlorinated to be potable, or drinkable. Yet of the 80 gallons of water used by the typical American, only one-quarter of a gallon is consumed by drinking. That leaves 79.75 gallons for flushing (22 gallons), washing clothes and dishes (20 gallons), bathing (24 gallons) and miscellaneous faucet running, for example for the entire time one is brushing one's teeth (10 gallons) -- oh, and leaking toilets (four gallons). 38

We should take note of the fact that using a gallon of water is not the same thing as using a gallon of gasoline. Once used, the gasoline is gone, broken down into constituent elements and dispersed. But no matter what you do with the water -- boil it, digest it, flush it, whatever (with a few exceptions) -- it's still water, still in the hydrological cycle. The sum total of water never changes. What changes is the amount of water available to us for the particular uses we regard as critical at a given time.

One effect of the over-processing of public water is excessive use of chlorine, which is also used in massive quantities to disinfect the used water before it is dumped into a river. Chlorine is extraordinarily beneficial in some of its forms and exceptionally toxic in others. The chloride ion in salt, for example, is essential to human biochemistry; without it, food cannot be digested and the body's proper water content cannot be maintained. Chlorine is an integral part of civilized summertime life -- it disinfects swimming pools. In its green gaseous form it also kills on contact, as demonstrated by Fritz Haber in the World War I

37 www.waterencyclopedia.com/Po-Re/Pricing-Water.html
38 Purdue University: www.purdue.edu/envirosoft/groundwater/src/ supply.htm#home. USGS: http://pubs.usgs.gov/circ/2004/circ1268/

trenches of Ypres and by the occasional hapless pool-maintenance person. Chlorine compounds are everywhere -- they bleach our laundry and our paper, kill pesky bugs and weeds, sedate us for surgery, disinfect our bathrooms and our wounds, surround us with plastic gizmos, dissolve just about anything metallic. Few substances other than petroleum are as ubiquitous in consumer products as is chlorine.

Chlorine consumption is, in fact, an index of the health of industry and of the sickness of our planet. Chlorine combines with carbon to form some of the most toxic, destructive and persistent substances on earth, including the pesticide DDT that nearly destroyed the bottom of our food chain, the chlorofluorocarbons (CFCs) that nearly wiped out the ozone layer, and such other bad actors as PCBs and Dioxin, increasingly linked not only to cancer, but to disastrous hormonal and immunological changes in wildlife and humans. These compounds are found in traces so small as to be virtually unmeasurable, and act so slowly their full impact may not be known for generations. Instead of poisoning or causing cancer, they imitate the natural hormones of living bodies well enough to take over, and then sabotage, the many functions that hormones control. Accumulating over months and years in exposed individuals -- over generations in exposed populations -- and becoming more concentrated as they move up the food chain, these substances eventually cause vast, irreversible harm, especially to the immune, reproductive and endocrine systems, especially to the young and drastically to the unborn.

The threat to wildlife was documented a decade ago by the US-Canadian International Joint Commission, which reported that of 42 compounds known to be afflicting the reproductive or hormone systems of living things in on and near the Lakes -- infertile eggs, deformed offspring, birds abandoning their young, fish swimming upside-down -- more than half "contain chlorine as an essential ingredient." In one Florida lake, 75 per cent of the eggs laid by alligators exposed to a DDT spill were infertile.

In humans, various studies have linked chlorine-based chemicals to a worldwide decline in fertility (sperm counts) and increase in testicular cancer in men, and to an increase of breast cancer and endometriosis in women. In 1994 the National Institutes of Health devoted a full conference to the threats, and the Clinton administration proposed a "national strategy for substituting, reducing or prohibiting the use of chlorine and chlorinated compounds." The Chlorine Chemistry Council responded with charges that critics of their products were not using "a sound-science approach to decision-making," were threatening 1.3 million American jobs, and were attacking "one of the most significant public-health advances of the 20th Century."

Take a Leak. Any leak.

Another effect of the politically mandated under-pricing of public water is a chronic neglect of aging water lines and processing plants. Consider the plight of New York City. Nowhere in the world is industrial water more gargantuan, or more beset by worsening problems, than in Gotham City. Using an array of surface reservoirs in the mountains west and north of the city, connected by a 125-mile-long network of aqueducts, the city delivers 1.2 billion gallons per day of water that is famous for its taste and purity. But that fame is beginning to slip away as the aging system (its oldest components are over 165 years old, its youngest 40 years) gradually succumbs to time and an array of threats.

It leaks. One of its tunnels -- the 45-mile-long, 13.5-foot-diameter Rondout-West Branch tunnel, conduit for half the city's water, was finished in 1944 and expected to last a hundred years. But for 20 years it has been leaking 20 million gallons a day, recently up to 36 million gallons a day. The city is spending a quarter of a billion dollars trying to fix it with divers without interrupting service. Try to imagine New York without half its water for a matter of months. [39]

---

39 "Plumber's Job on a Giant's Scale: Fixing New York's Drinking Straw."

There are also grave problems affecting the quality of water being taken from the reservoirs. For more than a century the city has been aggressive in acquiring and then protecting reservoirs and their watersheds, and it is not slowing down. Just in the last ten years the city has bought 70,000 acres upstate at a cost of $168 million, a pace it expects to continue. Just to pay the property taxes on its water-related land holdings costs the city over $100 million a year. Nevertheless, rampant development in the various watersheds, combined with more frequent and more violent rainstorms associated with climate change, resulted by the summer of 2006 in severe turbidity -- a fancy word for muddy water. Silt suspended in drinking water is more than an aesthetic problem, it interferes with chlorination.

To clear the way for the application of one toxic chemical, chlorine, the city began applying another -- hydrous aluminum potassium sulfate, or alum -- up to 16 tons a day on average in 2006 -- to settle out the dirt. The only other way to meet federal water standards would be to filter the water, and a plant big enough to do that for New York would cost something north of eight billion dollars and take a decade to build. On the other hand, the alum continues to accumulate as a toxic sludge on the bottoms of the reservoirs, killing aquatic life and demanding eventual dredging.[40]

New York's impending water crisis is far from unique. Some of Philadelphia's water mains are made of wood and more than 200 years old. According to the US Environmental Protection Agency, there are 240,000 water-main breaks in the country every year – in 2003, the city of Baltimore had about three *per day*.[41] The city of Warren, Michigan, may not be typical, but it is emblematic: in the winter of 2008-9, it suffered 107 water-main

New York Times 11/23/2008
40 "New York's Water Supply May Need Filtering." *New York Times* 07/20/2006
41 US EPA Aging Water Infrastructure Research Program, www.epa.gov/nrmrl/pubs/600f07015/600f07015.pdf

breaks in one month, one of which cut off water to a major shopping center and formed a sinkhole that ate a van.[42] As we come ever closer to the absolute limits of our water supplies, we are losing an estimated 1.7 trillion gallons of treated, potable water through leaks in ancient pipes.

Water for Food

As severe as are the demands for drinking water on the depleted water resources of the country, they pale in comparison with the demands of industrial agriculture. With its appetite for large-scale operations on marginal land – the same appetite that caused the Dust Bowl by plowing arid land – and its faith in technology, the industry quaffs water with breathtaking abandon. According to the USGS, 65% of the water withdrawn from all sources since 1950 has been used for irrigation. By contrast, withdrawals for all public water supplies in 2000 amounted to only 11 per cent of the total.[43] As supplies look more and more restricted, the friction between farm and city for what remains, increases.

California is the poster state for water disputes because of its huge population, densely clustered in urban areas far from their water supplies, and because of its huge agriculture industry. California agriculture was mostly created by industry, there was no previous expanse of diversified farms, for the simple reason that much of California's cropland – the southern half of the enormous Central Valley and the entirety of the Imperial Valley – is desert. The Imperial Valley, on California's border with Mexico, was so dry, hot and hostile that early Spanish explorers called it the Valley of the Dead. Although it gets only three inches of rainfall a year, it is today a major source of this country's fruits and vegetables, of which it grows two crops a year. These thirsty plants flourish

---

42 "Aging of Water Mains Hard to Ignore." *New York Times*
43 "Estimated Use of Water in the Unites States in 2000":
    http://pubs.usgs.gov/circ/2004/circ1268/htdocs/text-total.html

thanks to the water of the Colorado River – whatever amount escapes the clutches of Las Vegas – which is captured just before it escapes into Mexico by the All American Canal. The Canal takes it 80 miles east, along and just north of the border, to be distributed throughout the Valley by 2,500 miles of canals and pipelines.

Similarly, California's Central Valley, much of which is technically a desert, is another of the nation's leading sources of lettuce, tomatoes, almonds, grapes, melons, broccoli, cauliflower, wheat, onions, and garlic. (Lettuce, a friend once observed, is California's way of exporting water to the world. From a desert.) Fresno County, in the heart of the Central Valley's driest area and of a drought disaster area declared in 2008, claims to be is the largest agricultural county in the US, based on its production of $4.8 billion worth of crops per year.

As climate change has diminished the annual snow pack on the Sierra Mountains, whose melting swells the rivers of California every spring, and has inflicted worsening and lengthening drought on the entire American Southwest, industrial agriculture has gone underground for its water.

Water Under Cover

We are all dimly aware of water impoundments such as Lakes Mead and Lanier, if for no other reason than that we run around on them with our boats. But 95 per cent of our fresh water is invisible, pooled deep in the earth in underground reservoirs -- really more like soaked sponges than lakes -- called aquifers.

The largest of these in the United States, and one of the largest in the world, is the Ogallala aquifer that lies under eight states from South Dakota in the north to New Mexico and Texas in the south. With an area of 174,000 square miles, its top between 100 feet and 400 feet underground, and its thickness ranging from a few feet to several hundred feet, the Ogallala provides the drinking water for virtually everyone who lives above it. If that were the only demand made of it, we would not yet have cause to worry. But the aquifer also provides 30 per cent of all the groundwater used in irrigation in this country.

The water in the Ogallala is for the most part fossil water, which is to say it was deposited there a very long time ago, during the last Ice Age, which ended 10,000 years ago. Some replenishment water manages to trickle though the overlying earth, but very slowly. Our resources of fossil water are very nearly as finite and limited as our fossil fuels.

Since the 1950s, the industrial farmers of the Great Plains have gone after the water of the Ogallala as if it were inexhaustible, sucking it up with huge electric pumps to drench their crops through huge, center-pivot irrigation booms. At some places the water table in the aquifer dropped more than five feet per year at the time of maximum extraction, while replenishment of the water was measured in fractions of an inch per year. In many areas, wells have had to be extended to reach the steadily falling water table, and in some places such as Northern Texas, there is no more water to be reached. Today, water continues to be extracted at rates exceeding one hundred times the natural replacement rate.

The fundamental laws under which nature operates are not difficult to understand. One of them is: if you take stuff out of a container faster than you put stuff into the container, at some point the container will have no more stuff in it. There have always been droughts, and changes in climate, and they are not the cause of the increasing danger to our water supply any more than they are to blame for the coming oil shortages or food shortages. The fault, as Shakespeare said, is not in our stars (nor in our atmosphere) but in ourselves.

Chapter Four: Waste Water, Want Water

We were shown the way to stop polluting our water in 1969, a few years after the Cuyahoga River caught fire and ignited a national sense of revulsion at what we had done, and of urgency to change our ways. One man showed us how to do it, so convincingly that in 1972 the US Congress passed, and President Richard Nixon signed (after his veto was overturned by a *unanimous* vote of the Senate), legislation embodying the solution and confidently proclaiming as a national goal that *the discharge of all pollutants into the waters of the United States would cease by 1985.*

It was no pipe dream. It was reasonable to expect, based on what that one man showed us, that we could with little effort and with substantial additional benefits stop polluting our water. Period. The story of how the solution was presented to us, and how the people who run our country refused it, embodies every aspect of our imminent ruination: the wretched excesses of our prosperity; the ingenuity of which we are capable in devising ways to live more lightly on the land; and the brute power of greed to extinguish ingenuity in order to perpetuate profits.

Muskegon Blues

Muskegon, Michigan in 1965 could have replaced Cleveland, with its Cuyahoga River, as the poster city for America's nascent environmental movement. Like most American cities, it was paying a heavy price for having embraced the Industrial Revolution -- tree cutters, oil-well drillers, iron smelters and factory builders had brought prosperity and left a ruin. Looking back on it three decades later, Rod Ditmer wondered why he took the job that year as Muskegon County's planning director. He was expected to bring hope to a place that had been devastated by industrial exploitation and health to a city in the throes of an ugly, septic death. "I guess I was kind of young and foolish," he told me a few years ago, "and thought I could do anything."

Rod Ditmer could see, under all the industrial grime, that Muskegon was worth fighting for: "The town site had tremendous natural assets." Located midway along the western coast of the state's thumb-shaped Lower Peninsula, the city looked out over wide white beaches to the waters of Lake Michigan to westward, and over Muskegon Lake to the north. "It had a wildlife refuge that came right into the heart of the urban metropolitan area, several state parks, it just had a number of things going for it in terms of its natural disposition."

At this point in recounting what he confronted, Ditmer sighed: "But there was also a history of resource exploitation." Indeed. It had started in the 1820s when fur trappers pretty well cleared the area of small animals. It had accelerated in the 1870s when loggers deforested western Michigan to rebuild Chicago after the great fire of 1871. Toward the turn of the century some 30 keening sawmills lined the lake shore, and Muskegon was known as Sawmill City. But it was in the first half of the 20th Century that the exploitation became truly awesome.

There was oil and gas to be had in western Michigan and the folks who came to get it were not environmentalists: "they kind of overproduced," as the ever-understated Ditmer put it, "and didn't do a real good job of drilling and developing the oil wells." Then there were the iron foundries that capitalized on the Lake Michigan sand dunes, and devastated those. The sand -- in beaches along the lakes, in great drifted dunes along the shore of Lake Michigan, and in a layer 300 feet deep between the surface and the bedrock of Muskegon County -- was the gift of the glaciers that had excavated Lake Michigan, enlarging it from a round pond up near Green Bay into the massive digit that now reaches along the length of Michigan to tap Indiana on one shoulder. The plutocrats of pig iron needed sand in which to cast their iron pigs, so they took it by the thousands of tons, while casting a pall of black smoke over the city with their furnaces. Diplomacy deserted Ditmer as he groped for a word to describe that perpetual shroud: "it was really, just -- appalling."

The water was no better. "You could stick a paddle into the lake, and 12 inches down you couldn't see the paddle. It was really bad. Scott Paper was pouring out about 12 million gallons of effluent per day into the lake -- you could see the plume on aerial photos." Add to that the effluent from 160,000 urban dwellers and a phalanx of heavy industries -- not just the paper mill, but petroleum refineries, chemical plants and manufacturers of automobile parts, furniture and machinery -- and you had well over 40 million gallons of dirty and contaminated water per day (nearly 90 million gallons on a peak day) gushing through four aged municipal sewage treatment plants.

Meanwhile the area was in deepening economic recession. Businesses and manufacturers were leaving and failing, and there was nothing to take their place as employers and taxpayers. Agriculture in the area was moribund and tourism could not prosper on the fouled waters of the Muskegon River and Lake

Michigan. Boarded-up storefronts, empty warehouses and forests of aging "for-sale" signs told the story of a town on the skids, of the onset of industrial rigor mortis.

The condition was complicated by political paralysis. The county board was an amalgam of 53 representatives of the county's 17 cities, towns and townships. Their deliberations constituted a continuous floating turf fight, with the townships battling each other whenever they were not combining to fight a town or city. No one spoke for or represented the entire county. When Ditmer came on board as planning director for this group in 1965, the former board chairman took him aside and murmured the key to success: "Don't do any more than necessary. And don't spend any money."

Tilting at Sewage Mills

Something had to be done about Muskegon's misery. And Rod Ditmer knew that he, with no budget and a staff consisting of one secretary, was the one who had to do it. What is more, he believed he could do it -- if only he could get a clear picture of what he was dealing with. He needed data on where people were living, how old they were, how much education they had, what they wanted; and on the state of the county's infrastructure, the roads and rails and resources available to support life and commerce. He needed maps: of land uses, soil types, drainage areas, elevations and slopes.

If he could get the data and the maps, he would need help analyzing and interpreting them, in finding a way out of the awful mess in which the county found itself. He went to Michigan State University, taking with him into the ivory towers a whiff of political brimstone, of problems not subject to easy, neat or detached solutions. There was no help for him there: "They were concerned they might get burned." Only one professor cleared his throat and wondered whether it might behoove a state-supported university to put a shoulder to some of the state's serious problems, but he was quickly silenced.

Ditmer went to the US Geological Survey, whose primary mission at the time was the long process of working up maps and studies of the water resources of each county in the country, and asked the agency to do Muskegon right away. Sure, said the USGS managers, they would take Muskegon out of order. For $250,000. Ditmer kept on shopping.

"I hate to tell you where I got the money." One government program was throwing cash at localities in the mid-1960s (as the US Department of Homeland Security would be doing 40 years later), preparing the country to survive nuclear war by investing heavily in such things as pre-planned and -mapped evacuation routes; public bomb shelters; get-under-your-school-desk air-raid drills; frequent, hair-raising tests of imminent-attack sirens; and screw-your-neighbor backyard bomb shelters. Ditmer couldn't remember the official designation because he and his colleagues always called it the Love the Bomb program. Ditmer loved the program. It gave him the money he needed for the aerial photography, mapping and population studies he needed to start planning his way out of a different kind of Armageddon.

Even as Ditmer was getting started, time was running out. Lashed into action by a horrified public, state and federal governments were establishing and enforcing controls on pollution. Where the water was concerned, these limits were designed not to solve the problem, but to slow its worsening. In general, the regulators were insisting that every municipality give its sewage at least secondary treatment.

The Solution to Pollution is Dilution

Sewage, as a well-known brand of soap used to claim, is 99.9 per cent pure. That's how much of it is just water. The devil, in this case, is in the remaining thousandth part. That's where you find the bacteria, viruses and parasites that cause diseases; the solids -- floating, suspended, dissolved or colloidal -- that lend smell and color to the water; and various chemicals of varying toxicity.

Most cities in America, in the mid-1960s, were giving their wastewater only rudimentary treatment. Today, this minimalist approach is called "primary," as contrasted with "secondary" and "tertiary," or "advanced" wastewater treatment. In the words of a water-quality activist of the time, primary sewage treatment consisted of removing the "bowling balls and dead bodies." The collected flow from sinks, toilets and drains was run through grates and screens to remove the big stuff, then held in tanks long enough for the heavy stuff that remained to settle to the bottom and the floating stuff to be skimmed off. Primary treatment concluded with a dose of the sewermeister's wonder drug: chlorine. This is the chemical that made modern sewage treatment possible by preventing people from dying in windrows from cholera, typhus and the other plagues that attend accumulations of untreated excreta.

The product of primary sewage treatment is very dirty water. It still contains about half of the solid organic compounds -- the byproducts of living processes, such as digestion, that are suspended or dissolved in raw sewage -- that it carried to the sewage plant. These solids not only cloud the water, they cause a population explosion of the microorganisms that feed on them. These microorganisms require oxygen, which they take from the water, depleting the supply available for other forms of life such as fish. Biochemical oxygen demand, or BOD, is a standard measure of water pollution, indicating the degree to which the effluent strangles other living things in the water. To get BOD down, you have to go to secondary sewage treatment.

Secondary treatment is a biological, rather than a chemical, process. If you give those microorganisms a place to hang out and supply them with enough time and oxygen, they will eat the organic solids right out of that wastewater. But creating those conditions is far from easy. If, for example, you had been putting all of Muskegon's wastewater through one plant in the late 1960s, you would have been contending with nearly two million gallons of wastewater per hour. Since the bacteria need at least two hours

100

to make a dent in the organic content, the first thing you would need to keep up with that flow would be a tank big enough to hold two hours' worth -- about four million gallons. The second need is for oxygen. That's what it's all about, remember, biological oxygen demand, and to fill that demand this four million gallons of water would have to be aerated -- constantly bubbled with injected air.

Nor is that all. Given time and air, those bacteria spend their whole lives eating organic compounds and then, bless them, they die, and their little bacteria bodies sink in the water, by the billions. That's what sludge is. (Sewermeisters like to let us assume that sludge is what they're taking out of the sewage but it is not; it is what they are growing in order to keep the flow going.) You have to get the bacteria bodies out of the water because, after all, they are simply a different kind of water pollution. So, to achieve secondary treatment, you have to have another tank, called a clarifier, in which you can hold the water for two or three more hours while the bodies settle out. Now you can disinfect the clarified water and dump it in the river.

But you have created another set of problems. You have to do something with the thickened water (or, if you prefer, the thin sludge) drawn from the bottom of the clarifier. It's got too many solids in it to dump, and too much water to bury. So you reduce the solids, which are by now mostly bacteria bodies, by having another kind of bacteria (the anaerobic kind, which can't stand oxygen) digest them again. For this, and for the thickened solids to settle out, you have to have yet another huge tank, the digester, and when you take the thick soup out of the digester and dry it out you have one ton of dry organic matter for every million gallons of wastewater you have treated. In Muskegon that would have meant nearly two tons of dry sludge an hour, maybe 50 tons every day, and you have to do something with that. Like put it in the landfill, which is already filling up way too fast.

Anyway, that's what the feds and the state were now telling Muskegon to do: get those little critters working and get the organic solids out of your wastewater. But upgrading all four Muskegon plants with the necessary tanks, pumps and plumbing would cost hundreds of millions of dollars, quadrupling everyone's sewer fees, and would mean only that the water quality of the region would not get much worse, but neither would it get better, and thus no economic growth in Muskegon would be possible.

In fact, the plutocrats of pig iron, leather and paper, who had trained a generation of politicians to regard sooty skies and foul water as the price of progress, were leaving, taking with them the payrolls and tax revenues that Muskegon had bought and paid for with its air and water. Even Scott Paper, with a thousand jobs the area's largest employer, was talking about closing down. The old-line politicians had found themselves, like aging whores, still willing to sell anything, but increasingly without takers. When that happens, it's time to develop a new skill.

Rod Ditmer's job description changed from "don't do any more than necessary," to "do something!" But although the political will had appeared, the machinery of government was pretty creaky. "The county had no history of public works other than rural drainage projects," Ditmer said. "My pitch to the county board and the local units of government was that we're not going to consolidate all these units, so why not move toward functional consolidation?" Surprisingly, the contentious localities were soon able to agree on the need for one sewage treatment plant in the metropolitan area. That meant there were three that were going to have to be abandoned. And they all were carrying debt. It would be like putting a car up on blocks in your back yard while you were still making payments. It went against nature.

"I heard about this guy Jack Sheaffer, with the Institute of Urban Studies at the University of Chicago, who had a reputation for driving everybody up the wall. He was telling the suburbs to stop sucking on Chicago's straw and develop their own stable, long-term water supplies so they could keep their political independence. And he was working on a plan for handling

Chicago's sludge with abandoned oil pipelines. "I went to hear him speak at a conference in Milwaukee. He was talking to an audience of engineers and bureaucrats, and he was just giving them hell. I walked in to the back of the room a few minutes after he started, and I could see that the back of every neck in the room was already deep red."

"Someone suggested I go to Jack Sheaffer for help with our water resource management, and I said, 'Oh, my God. We'd be in for a hell of a fight.'"

The Flood Guy

When I met him in the 1990s, Dr. John R. "Jack" Sheaffer was a slight, elfin man with a thatch of white hair and a permanently hoarse voice. His eyes gleamed with the barely contained amusement of an uncle who has posed a riddle to his nephews and nieces, and is watching them struggle while he withholds the simple answer. His favorite thing in life is the moment when he reveals the answer, and sees the looks of amazement.

In 1969 he was about 40, but looked much younger. He was by then fully immersed in the welter of intellectual pursuits that characterized his life. Having completed his doctoral degree in geography at the University of Chicago, he had joined the University's Institute of Urban Studies. There, in addition to teaching, he was serving on a Public Health Service advisory committee that apportioned grant money; as director of the Lake Michigan and Adjoining Land Study Commission, created by the Illinois General Assembly to create a "bill of rights" for Lake Michigan; a consultant to the US Army Corps of Engineers; and as a member of a blue-ribbon commission set up by New York Mayor John Lindsay to deal with the worst garbage-collection mess the country had yet seen. His doctoral dissertation on flood proofing served as a template for national, state, and local regulations on this topic, including the national flood insurance program.

"I was always regarded as a flood man," says Sheaffer. While the Corps of Engineers drew on his knowledge of flood control, the Public Health Service directed his attention to matters of water supply, solid waste disposal and sewage treatment. As he pursued these assignments, he kept running into something that made no sense to him -- sewage treatment plants built on flood plains. "I would say to people, 'why do you put this pile of junk on the flood plain? You know it's going to be flooded, there's going to be raw sewage in the river.' And they would say that that was the only place you could put them. Well that was just too much of a challenge."

It was immediately clear to him, as it had become to Ditmer, that water was at the heart of all of Muskegon's problems, and held the key to its future. "Muskegon was a pretty dismal town," he remembered. "Really bleak. It had these dune-impounded lakes that could be a really nice feature, but they were filthy. You couldn't see two inches into the water. Muskegon County had no recreational dollars coming in and no agriculture, and these were the two dominant things in Michigan. It had a lot of dirty industry, polluted water, and a lot of low productivity land." Eager to get his hands on Muskegon, the town that had everything, Sheaffer signed on to work up a water resource policy to guide the area's redevelopment.

Jack Sheaffer's brain is about as quiet as the night sky over Washington DC on Independence Day. Ideas flare and crackle in there constantly, with an occasional great flowering burst, now and then a dud, and every once in a while an accidental explosion on the ground. So perhaps it is not surprising that he does not remember any particular epiphany about sewage treatment, no opportunity to shout "Eureka" in the bathtub.

Another reason he does not recall working it out is that it was all so bloody obvious. As he had looked at where water came from, and where it went, Sheaffer had begun to say three things over and over, in what would become the *mantra* of his life. "The

104

environment is a closed system." Translation: nothing comes in or goes out, so you have to make do with the resources you have. The second axiom was a close corollary of the first: "Everything goes someplace." Since whatever you throw away remains in the system, sending waste downstream or downwind simply moves the problem into another neighborhood. The responsible thing is to deal with your own waste where you create it. These were theoretical statements, but his third principle had economic muscle -- and fateful implications. "Pollution is just a resource out of place."

Questions determine their answers. If you ask: How do I get rid of this waste? you will think about getting it out of sight, dumping it, burying it, letting the devil take it downstream. If you ask instead: How do I get this resource to the place where it is most valuable? different things come to mind. Thus when Sheaffer went to Muskegon he saw a town that was strangling its lakes, and hence its tourist business, with nutrients at the same time its agriculture was languishing for lack of *those same nutrients*. In order to avoid discharging more unwanted nutrients into the water, it was choking its industry and its growth. The answer was obvious and simple -- take the nutrients out of the water and put them on the land, thus using the pollution to grow cash crops.

Simple, maybe, but far from easy. Muskegon's towns, cities and industries had millions invested in getting rid of their wastewater, and were firmly entrenched behind one of the most enervating defenses in human history: we've always done it this way. But Sheaffer had been thinking about these things ever since they told him that the only place you could put a sewage treatment plant was a floodplain. In that great division of human thinkers between generalists and specialists, he is a generalist, who begins by throwing his net wide across many disciplines and deep into history. This is the way he finds truths that can survive outside their specialties and beyond their time.

History was instructive. Go back too far and you're out of

range, because sewage is not a problem for the hunter-gatherer, the nomad, the farmer, even the town-dweller. You have to be in a town of substantial size and density before you have a sewage problem. Even then, what constitutes a problem for the townhouse-dweller is a solution for the farmer; it consists, after all, primarily of things that improve soil and nourish plants. As the world became more citified, it began to displace its urban sewage, but just a little at first. -- to farms outside the city center that were able to apply the grossest domestic product, as it were, to growing crops.

The city of Paris has been using raw sewage to fertilize fields of vegetables since 1883. During the second half of the 19th Century, sewage farms operated outside Berlin, Edinburgh, London, Manchester and dozens of other European cities. Outside Melbourne, Australia, raw sewage was applied to pasture land, fertilizing grass for consumption by beef cattle. In fact, at the time Sheaffer began his investigation, about a thousand *American* communities were applying sewage (usually after primary treatment) to cropland. People were using wastewater as a resource, but they were not good neighbors. Their fertilizer has a terrible odor, and they often spread it when it was raining, or when the ground was frozen, with the result that it ran off into streams and onto others' land.

But what killed most of the urban sewage farms was not their nastiness. What killed them was the rise of the fertilizer industry (initially on the backs of guano-mining peasants in Peru and Chile), which made commercial fertilizer cheaper and easier to apply than sewage; the rise of real estate values, in step with the increase in population density, making that urban farm far too valuable to be used for sewage, or, for that matter, for farming; and, above all, the realization that if you dumped sewage in a river, it went away.

Sheaffer knew that even if economics changed to the extent that you could bulldoze a few acres of row houses to make use of the land, you could not go back to the old sewage farms. If you took care of the odor and health problems inherent in raw sewage, you could use the nutrients, but they would have to be applied at a rate and during those times that growing plants could make use of them. Since 1962, scientists at Pennsylvania State University had been conducting trials of the effects of applying secondary effluent to forests, old fields and cropland. They found that if you managed carefully the amounts of nitrogen and water you released to growing plants, "it should be possible," in the words of the program's managers, "to recharge water of drinking quality into the aquifer below a wastewater disposal site."

Pollution Becomes a Solution

Food for thought here. This was not raw-sewage farming as of old, this was making use of effluent that had been disinfected, strained, and settled. All that was required to bring that water to drinking-water quality was the presence of growing plants. Oh, and one more thing -- someplace to put the water when the ground was frozen, or saturated with rain. In Michigan, that could mean almost half the year. Any engineer whose mind so much as flicked at this idea would chuckle and move on, but Jack Sheaffer was not a water-treatment guy, he was a flood guy. "To store 100 million gallons of water for six months, that only takes a modest size flood control reservoir. But a sanitary engineer could not imagine a concrete tub that big."

This was the really big idea. It sprang naturally from regarding the wastewater as a resource. If it was just waste you piped it away, dosed it with chemicals and dumped it. But if it was a resource, like oil or gas, then you invested in a place to hoard it, so you can use it as you need it. What you would be doing could no longer be sewage disposal, it would be wastewater recycling.

So here's the concept Sheaffer enunciated to Muskegon. Take all your wastewater and pipe it to the edge not of a lake or river, but of a corn field. Grind it, disinfect it, run it through screens and pump it into into the bottom of a holding cell – a huge pond. There, the smelly work of sewage treatment is done; the digestion of the organic content into methane, carbon dioxide, hydrogen sulfide and water. This is done in the absence of oxygen. But stand next to this pond and you will smell nothing, because three feet up from the bottom, the Sheaffer system injects compressed air, fully aerating the top layer of the water so that oxygen-loving microbes and the processes of oxidization eliminate the noxious smells associated with sewage. Because this system gives the microbes the time and the conditions they need to do their work there is no need to stimulate their growth artificially, and hence virtually no accumulation of sludge. After 18 days in the first of these treatment cells, the water spends 12 days in a second and then, if it's winter or it's wet, is moved to a reservoir (Muskegon's reservoir was capable of holding 151 days' worth of sewage.) During the growing season this rich brew of water and nutrients is used to irrigate corn, or any other valuable crop. While the roots of the corn take up the nutrients, the soil and its microorganisms filter out and make use of any remaining organic chemicals or suspended solids. By the time the mixture has worked its way a foot or so down into the soil, it is as pure as water gets. So here is a credentialed engineer with a national reputation, hired by a city to save it, announcing that he had designed the solution. When the county chairman explained Sheaffer's plan to what was then called the Federal Water Pollution Control Administration, as Sheaffer recalled it, "They practically hit him on the head with a chair and threw him out in the street. They told him get out of here this is irresponsible. That was one of the shocks of my life. I really thought that people who were working with water quality wanted to see that water clean. And they didn't. They wanted to maintain the status quo."

It was not merely that people doubted that Sheaffer could deliver. It was that too many people had too much time and money invested in the status quo. Engineering firms, contracting firms, concrete and chlorine suppliers and the like all knew exactly how to get rich building sewage treatment plants that did not work. Why would they be interested in building something that would work?

"They said to me look we're going to build this sewage treatment plant, and I said well it is going to give us clean water? And they said well no, but it won't get any worse and I said how conceivably could it be any worse than it is? You can't see two inches into the water, there's no fishing, it's viewed as a detriment rather than an asset.

"The thing that shocked me even more than that was the attitude of the environmental groups. In Muskegon there was a group, Save Our Lake, and they met and they would issue stormy things about water quality of Muskegon Lake so I thought man, here's some helpers. I went to them and said I'm going to propose that we take all the waste water out of Muskegon Lake and make it clean. These guys attacked me with viciousness. You'll destroy all the jobs. You can't do that, you'll drive industry out of this town, why, we'll all be unemployed. I couldn't believe it. Two guys there had a big article in *Life* Magazine, writing them up as the leaders in the quest for clean water. They actually sued to prevent the project. We showed them you can succeed, they didn't want to."

Despite the friends of the people and of the environment, Jack Sheaffer built the Muskegon Miracle. It went on line in 1972 and performed exactly as he said it would (although to be sure he later made improvements to his system and wished that they had been part of the Muskegon system). More importantly, it proved beyond the shadow of doubt that we could reclaim and reuse the nastiest sewage the industrial age could produce, at the volumes generated by a substantial city (40 million gallons per day), and restore it to purity without discharging any pollutants to water, ground or air. All we needed to do was set aside a little ground for growing things.

1972 was a triumphal year for Jack Sheaffer. Since 1970 he had been serving as science adviser to the Secretary of the Army and in that capacity had helped write the legislation that would become the Clean Water Act revisions of 1972. With the Senate's unanimous override of Nixon's veto, the Congress proclaimed to the country that Jack Sheaffer had solved the problem of water pollution and that within a few years it would be only a memory of a more primitive time. And then Jack Sheaffer and his water reclamation system dropped from national view and were seldom heard from again.

He soldiered on, of course. During the next four decades he installed more than 100 systems for reclaiming and reusing water, but every one of them was achieved only by a to-the-death, no-holds-barred cage fight with Jack Sheaffer on one side and on the other the massed forces of all the engineers, consultants, concrete-pourers, pipe-fitters, chlorine merchants and we've-always-done-it-this-way politicians who were invested in the successful business of building failed sewage plants.

Still, it would have been a fair fight had it not been for one other thing. After Sheaffer got past the skepticism, the deep and not unreasonable feeling that what sounds too good to be true might not be true; after he bested the stiff and well-financed resistance of the potential losers of fat contracts; the unstoppable Sheaffer met the unmovable object of the modern American political and economic system -- the developers.

The things that killed the Sheaffer vision of no more water pollution in America was its requirement that a modicum of land be set aside for the growing plants that were an integral part of his system – and, by the way are the basis of the web of life on this planet. As he showed over and over again, this space is easily provided as parkland, golf courses, sports fields or cropland depending on the nature of the site. But the notion of putting any limitation whatsoever, for any reason, on the amount of land available for the development of quarter-acre McMansion develop-ments was unacceptable to the builders and developers who for nearly a half century now have been running America. With their ability to buy academic studies, saturation ad campaigns and politicians [*see Chapter Five: The Failed State*] and their appetite for two million acres a year, on average, of US land to put under asphalt, concrete and vinyl, the developers were an opponent that Sheaffer could defeat only now and then, only with great effort.

Sheaffer used to like to quote Victor Hugo: "invading armies can be resisted, but not an idea whose time has come." Apparently, Victor Hugo did not imagine the power of American land developers. They sank Sheaffer, they sank his idea, and they made a mockery of the national goal expressed with the full faith and credit of the United States Congress, to end all water pollution by 1985.

When You Miss the Water

Jack Sheaffer's story illustrates all the reasons for the imminent failure of industrial society. Whether we're talking about the supply of fresh water or the disposition of waste water, we see relentless exploitation of a limited, life-giving resource for profit. We see the implacable expansion – of irrigated acreage in deserts, of sewage plants on algae-clogged rivers – in search of economies of scale, with the real costs to real people, and the attendant concentration of graver and graver risks, well concealed.

In this area, as with agriculture – and, as we will see, as with petroleum and energy – smart people have figured out what the problems really are and, like Jack Sheaffer, have solved them. That's when, as Sheaffer found, two things happen. First, the very organizations and people who have been clamoring for a solution to the problem suddenly realize that an actual solution would put them out of business. A fund-raising letter that describes a crisis that's going to kill us all unless somebody does something, brings in a lot of money. One that says hey, that problem is solved, and we helped: not so much. How then will the activist organizations pay their staff salaries, maintain their elegant offices on K Street in Washington D.C., and support their lifestyles? Thus do the organizations that claim to be fighting problems end up clinging to them for dear life.

The second thing that happens is that the industries whose cash flows are threatened by the solution marshal their resources, which include their wholly-owned politicians, and they bury the proposed solutions under an avalanche of TV commercials, sponsored "studies" and craven speeches. Or, alternatively, the solutions simply wither with the passage of time. Money is especially adept at winning by waiting, by invoking every possible procedural delay, by bringing lawsuits and then seeking every available continuance, until their opponents go broke or die and the interested public becomes vagued out and distracted by some new scandal or diversion.

Their tactics have worked so well, and have so entrenched industrial water and wastewater in our society, that recovery from their excesses in time to sustain present population levels is not remotely possible. Only one thing now has the power to require such remedial actions as the abandonment of desert farmland over depleted aquifers, the bulldozing of townhouse developments to restore fields for growing food and reclaiming wastewater. And that one thing is the irreversible onset of collapse.

PART III. ENERGY

"Our ignorance is not so vast as our failure to use what we know."

M. King Hubbert

Chapter Five: The End of Oil

Congressman Roscoe Bartlett never looked like a prophet of doom when he took to the well of the House of Representatives to preview the downfall of the nation. A conservative Republican from western Maryland, in his 80s, he did not possess an imposing frame or demeanor, and although vigorous, moved with the somewhat tentative care required by his age. His views on such things as national security, taxes, gun rights and the like were mostly right-wing orthodox. But there was one surprising exception.

Over and over again, beginning in the spring of 2006 until his eventual defeat in 2012, he claimed hours of time to rail against the policies of a nation he said was hurtling toward disaster, in the form of a sudden, catastrophic end to the age of cheap and plentiful oil. That he spoke in the dry, careful tones of a research scientist (which in fact he had been for much of his life) made his message more believable than the average political speech -- and much less likely to appear on television news. His dissertations on these occasions, laden with statistics and illustrated with a multitude of complex graphs, resembled academic seminars more than speeches. Always they began by paying homage to M. King Hubbert, who had been a prophet of doom nearly a half century before Congressman Bartlett got into the prophet business.

Throwing a Curve

Dr. Hubbert had gone to work as a geologist for Shell Oil in 1943, and not long thereafter began to suspect, then confirmed by detailed observation and calculation, and then (to the dismay of his employers) announced, that America's supply of oil was not only limited, but would begin to run out in the foreseeable future, on a date he could predict. He laid out his case at the 1956 annual meeting of the American Petroleum Institute: He had found that every oil well, every oil field and in sum all the oil fields of the United States taken together, had a characteristic way of yielding their resources. At the beginning of production, the output of oil rose rapidly for a time, then leveled off and held steady for a while, then declined at about the same rate at which it had increased. When he charted the behavior, with time as the horizontal axis and yield as the vertical, he always got a fairly symmetrical, bell-shaped curve. The oilfields of the United States, Hubbert predicted, would reach their peak production and begin an irreversible decline about a decade after he spoke, or around 1970.

Two things about Hubbert's prediction cannot be overstated: the seriousness of its implications for a civilization that could not move or eat without cheap oil; and the scorn with which it was greeted. At the time, the United States was the largest producer, consumer and exporter of oil in the world, its production and consumption were rising rapidly, and no one was in a mood to imagine that the good times would ever end. Most people in, associated with, or beholden to the oil "bidness" (as they liked to say it in Houston, where he was speaking) regarded his prediction as beneath contempt, and did not speak of it at all. Consequently, few people outside the oil business ever heard about it. The good times continued, and about ten years later North America's largest oil field was discovered at Prudhoe Bay, Alaska. Take that,

Chicken Little!

Yet Hubbert's prediction was eerily exact. It is not even necessary to allow for the fact that his calculations were based on, and his prediction made for, the lower 48 states, not including Alaska. Because the Prudhoe field, for all its mammoth size -- about 25 billion barrels -- provided only a brief uptick on the down side of the US oil industry's long, inevitable slide toward zero that began, exactly as Hubbert predicted, in 1970.

Oil-Shock Absorbers

A rational response to the confirmation of Hubbert's Curve as predictor of the decline of oil production would have been near-panic. And that is what the country experienced three years later, not because of Hubbert's warning but because of the demonstration, by the Arab oil producers, of its eventual effect. The Organization of Petroleum-Exporting Countries (OPEC) embargoed oil exports to the United States, as retribution for American support of Israel in the Yom Kippur War. The embargo lasted only a few months, until the OPEC member countries began to miss the money. This brief reduction of about 10 per cent of supply, the effects of which were multiplied by clumsy government price controls and rationing, caused sharp price increases (oil quadrupled, to $12 per barrel, and gasoline went from 38 to 55 cents a gallon), long lines at gas stations, some regional shortages, a few near-riots, imposition of a national, 55-mile-per-hour speed limit and of year-round "daylight-saving time," and intense concern about energy-efficiency and -independence.

In 1974, Hubbert stepped briefly into the public square again. He was now employed by the US Geological Survey, his prediction of the peaking of US oil had been validated, and the Congress, seriously scared by the Arab oil embargo, had resolved that this should never come to pass again. It was cobbling together a national Energy Policy and Conservation Act, and asked Dr. Hubbert for his comments.

Patiently, Dr. Hubbert reviewed his findings about the fate of oil in the United States, and then delivered a death sentence for the Age of Oil, along with a date of execution:

"The peak in the production rate for the United States has already occurred three years ago in 1970. The peak in the production rate for the world based upon the high estimate of 2100 billion barrels, will occur about the year 2000. Without further elaboration, It is demonstrable that the exponential phase of the industrial growth which has dominated human activities during the last couple of centuries is drawing to a close." 44

A member of the committee hearing the testimony, Rep. Teno Roncalio of Wyoming (who four years later would earn a footnote in American history by relinquishing his seat to one Dick Cheney), managed to contain his astonishment. "Thank you very much," he said. "I would like to hear more some day."

The Congress contented itself with creating the grandly named Strategic Petroleum Reserve, a depository of a billion barrels of oil that would tide us over the next time the Arabs interfered with our supplies. Thereafter the Congress and the American people, despite the plea from President Jimmy Carter that achieving energy independence was "the moral equivalent of war," despite another wake-up call in the form of the second oil shock of 1979, despite credible warnings of impending disaster, packed all their stuff and moved permanently to the state of denial.

Count on It

In any discussion of the oil industry, as of climate change, agriculture, finance or any other subject that matters to the profits of large organizations and to the fate of humanity, we are cautioned to defer to experts. Just as many religions insist that only their priests can interpret God's will, so industrialists insist that

---

44 National Energy Policy Act of 1974, Hearings before the Subcommittee on the Environment, House Committee on Interior and Insular Affairs, June 6, 1974.

only their staff experts understand what industry is doing, and how good it is for the rest of us. Raise an objection, or even a question, and you will be told the matter is too complicated for ordinary people to consider.

Albert Einstein, who contemplated and interpreted the most complex ideas there are, did not feel that way. "Any intelligent fool can make things bigger, more complex, and more violent," he said. "It takes a touch of genius, and a lot of courage,,to move in the opposite direction." And he also said, "The whole of science is nothing more than a refinement of everyday thinking." So we can presume to have the blessing of Dr. Einstein in applying to this complicated business of oil and science of geology some everyday thinking, in order to move it toward smaller and simpler ideas.

Estimating the number of barrels of oil that remain in any well, field, or country, let alone the world, is a big and complex task. Let us begin instead with this small and simple truth: There is only so much oil on this planet. It and the "natural" gas often associated with it were formed only during two periods of extreme global warming, one 150 million years ago and another, 90 million years ago (Not for nothing is it called a "fossil" fuel). The oil is the residue of masses of algae that flourished in the world's warm seas and were subsequently, by glacially slow geological processes, buried and transformed deep underground (natural gas and coal were similarly formed from other vegetation) over many millions of years. How much there is altogether, no one knows, but everyone knows that there is only so much, and that it is not being replenished. Yet we all act, and plan our futures as if, it is never going to run out.

Birth of a Glutton

Its uses were limited when the world's first wells were brought in -- in Pennsylvania and on the shores of the Caspian Sea -- in the middle of the 19th Century. The Industrial Revolution was well under way on steam power, and large chunks of the country were being denuded of trees by the demand for wood to burn. Coal was a distant second as a source of energy. But with the invention of the internal combustion engine around 1860, its adaptation to the first automobiles in the 1880s and to farm tractors beginning in 1907, petroleum in the form of gasoline began to come into its own as a precious commodity. For half a century thereafter there was no reason to think about constraints or limits as new discoveries of oil, along with the development of existing fields, more than kept up with the world's rapidly increasing thirst for the stuff. A century later, in 2007, according to the CIA *World Fact Book*, the world consumed 85.25 million barrels of oil per day. According to *WorldOil.com*, in that year the world produced 85.25 million barrels of oil per day. That seems neat enough until you look at the trend lines -- demand shooting up just as it has for a hundred years, supply tailing off just as M. King Hubbert said it would.

It is well known that the United States by itself, with one twentieth of the world's population, guzzles one quarter of the world's oil supply, more than 20 million barrels of it every day. This long-standing fact has not led to any noticeable revulsion of feeling among the US population. Instead it has stimulated envy among the populations of China, India and other countries labeled as "emerging economies" -- meaning, presumably, that they are emerging from the dark night of sustainability into the bright light of suicidal gluttony. China, for example, was until 1993 an exporter of oil; now its dependence on uncertain supplies of foreign oil rivals that of the United States. Between 2002 and 2007, China's oil imports doubled, gobbling up 35 percent of the total increase in world oil consumption, and making it the number two consumer of oil in the world. It still has room for more emerging, however -- its 2007 rate of 7.5 million barrels a day was still just one-third of US consumption, even though Chinas had one billion more citizens than does the United States.

The global recession that began in 2008 put a serious crimp in the growth of demand for oil. The collapse of the casino economy, which its practitioners preferred to call investment banking, ensued after a welter of unbridled greed that lasted for at least two decades. While it lasted, players threw untold billions of borrowed money at imaginary assets, creating unsustainable bubbles of hysterical pricing based on the assumption that everything would increase in price forever. When the so-called dot-com bubble collapsed in 2000, the borrowed money began to slosh into other imaginary assets, such as sub-prime mortgages, derivatives and commodities futures.

Oil was one of those commodities, although to call it a commodity is in itself a mistake that leads to many other mistakes. A real commodity, such as corn, is produced by scalable human effort capable of responding to demand, which means that higher prices stimulate more production which lowers prices, and vice versa, a mechanism that in theory and sometimes in practice can regulate the market. Oil differs from this in a fundamental way: what we mean by oil "production" is the withdrawal of a portion of the oil that remains, an amount that is not being, and cannot be, increased. Thus while high prices for oil, such as those created by speculators gambling with oil futures in 2008, do have the effect of stimulating the "production" of non-conventional oil (tar sands, deep-water deposits, non-pressurized remnants and the like) too expensive to be profitable at lower prices, this effect does not change the underlying reality of a finite, irreplaceable and dwindling resource. And when an oil bubble collapses, as it did in 2008, lower prices depress "production" and increase demand, thus bringing ever nearer the consequences of that underlying reality.

Truth and Consequences

The exact amount of oil remaining in any field, let alone in all the fields in the world, is unknowable. It depends on so many variables of geology, of technological capability, economic reality and human ability, that certainty is beyond us. Moreover, if despite all the difficulties, a company or a country gets a pretty good idea of what's left in a field, the people who know the numbers are quite likely to keep them secret, or lie about them.

There are many motivations to lie. The larger the "proven" reserves announced, the more attractive the development of the field to the investors who must put up the staggering amounts of capital required. OPEC has traditionally assigned production quotas to its member countries that are proportional to their "proven" reserves. Therefor, if you are an oil minister, to inflate the estimate of your county's reserves is to increase your country's revenues. Moreover, if Big Oil admitted that it is running out of product, it would see a stampede to alternative energy sources that would hasten its fall from wealth and power. To be sure, in the face of slowly rising public awareness of the realities of oil, some companies such as British Petroleum have attempted to look like they are leading the way toward alternative solutions. But they have done so with advertising, not with commitment. Re-branding BP as "Beyond Petroleum," or airing Exxon commercials in which an elegant model assures us that everything is going to be all right, may affect public opinion but it does not affect the problem.

Just as in the debate over global climate change, the debate over the future of oil is filled with voices shouting facts at us, urging us to see the facts as they do, and belittling those who disagree. Mining the endless data for nuggets to support a preconceived view is easy, you never run out of raw material. But whom are we to believe?

In four decades of journalism, of interviewing people and gathering facts, always trying to determine not only whether the facts are true but what they mean, I have learned a few things about evaluating sources. I have learned to distrust people who are certain of their views on complex matters; people who know the answers before they hear the question; and people who always come out on the same side of an issue no matter what information comes before them. So I discount the arguments of oil experts and oil ministers whose employers' wealth depends on their opinions. (Exceptions, such as M. King Hubbert, are too few to be counted on.) Likewise I ignore the politicians who represent oil-rich states, and ignore all advertising.

There is one thing about truth, and recognizing truth, that goes beyond logical calculation. A person's knowledge and experience are cumulative, and yield over time more than an aggregation of factoids. One learns, slowly, that the truth has a subtle resonance, with all the other things you know and also perhaps with the universe itself. It has a clarity and consistency of tone quite different, to the attuned ear, from the clank and grind of lies.

One listens to the clamor, waiting for that clear tone, watching for that which moves away, as Einstein put it, from "things bigger, more complex, and more violent." One hopes especially for someone who speaks against his interests, as Dr. Hubbert did, as Congressman Bartlett does in declaring a national emergency to a Congress and to constituents who want only easy, comfortable answers. And the clarity is to be found in the too-little-known voices and writings of such as Richard Heinberg, Michael Klare, Matthew Simmons, Michael C. Ruppert, Julian Darley, Dr. Colin Campbell, Kenneth Deffeyes, and James Howard Kunstler.

This, then, is the consensus that emerges from the voices that appeal to everyday thinking. Never mind what the specific numbers and dates may be, because that way lies incessant wrangling over details that engages experts and loses the rest of us. Let's try to get the concepts right:

- We have used about half of all the oil that we can ever get -- and the second half of the oil in any well or field is the most difficult and expensive to extract.
- The global rate of consumption has been increasing rapidly, especially in China and India. The rate of increase was reduced by the global recession that began in 2008, but world demand nevertheless increased. US demand was more or less steady, but still disproportionately large.

The rate of discovery of new oil deposits has been declining since the 1960s. In every year since 1981, unlike every prior year of the age of oil, the world has consumed more oil than it has discovered. Figures available to the public indicate that the five major international oil companies have never exceeded their production achieved in 2004, and that Saudi Arabia, which possesses the largest depository of oil in the world, has not exceeded its production of April 2003.

These trends are not only persistent, they are accelerating.

It's Not the Stop. It's the Sudden Fall.

Despite the gravity of these trends, we could comfortably remain in a state of denial if the thing we had to worry about was running out of oil. By all accounts we have a century or more before that starts to happen. But long before there is no more oil, there will be peak oil, and the problems associated with that are nothing less than catastrophic.

To be clear about what peak oil is: to geologists, it's the point at which half a field's oil has been extracted, after which every barrel gets harder and more expensive to get. From a geopolitical point of view, peak oil can be thought of as the day on which world demand has increased, and world supply decreased, to the point that there is not enough oil available to fill existing orders. The moment the market understands that this is the case, several things will happen immediately. First, the price of all the remaining oil will increase exponentially. Second, all suppliers will be forced to choose between bidders based on factors other than price. Whether one sells to China or the United States, for example, will depend to a large degree on one's relations with and proximity to one country or the other -- or, more specifically, to their armed forces. Third, bidders whose citizens' welfare and governments' stability depends on oil will use whatever means they have to persuade sellers to take their offer. And as Al Capone once observed, "You can get a lot farther in this world with a smile and a gun, that you can with a smile."

What Do We Know and When Did We Know It?

In 2009, 35 years after Hubbert's prophetic testimony and Congressman Roncalio's dismissive remark about hearing more some day, the only voice from which Congress was hearing more about the rapidly approaching reckoning was the increasingly frail but maddeningly persistent Roscoe Bartlett.

Beginning in 2006, Bartlett had buttressed his own position by quoting from two reports commissioned, then ignored (actually, for a time apparently suppressed) by the US government. One, by the Energy Department -- which under the Bush Administration was little more than a cheerleader for the oil companies -- was titled "The Peaking of World Oil Production: Impacts, Mitigation and Risk Management," and was dated February, 2005. Among its conclusions:

- "The peaking of world oil production presents the United States and the world with an unprecedented risk management problem. As peaking is approached, liquid fuel prices and price volatility will increase dramatically, and without timely mitigation, the economic, social and political costs will be unprecedented."
- "Dealing with world oil production peaking will be extremely complex, involve literally trillions of dollars and require many years of intense effort."
- "The world has never faced a problem like this. Without massive mitigation more than a decade before the fact, the problem will be pervasive and will not be temporary. Previous energy transitions, wood to coal and coal to oil, were gradual and evolutionary. Oil peaking will be abrupt and revolutionary."

The second report Congressman Bartlett quoted *ad nauseum* to his fellow Representatives (or, more accurately, to the largely empty Capitol chamber where they would have been present, listening raptly, if they gave a damn) was commissioned by the US Army Corps of Engineers, was dated September of 2005

125

and titled: "Energy Trends and Their Implications For US Army Installations." A few of its observations:

- "The coming years will see significant increases in energy costs across the spectrum. Not only are energy costs an issue, but also reliability, availability, and security."
- "It is time to think strategically about energy and how the Army should respond to the global and national energy picture. A path of enlightened self-interest is encouraged. The 21st century is not the 20th century. Issues will play out differently and geopolitics will impact the energy posture of the Nation."
- "The days of inexpensive, convenient, abundant energy sources are quickly drawing to a close."

For years, Roscoe Bartlett, like an elderly Paul Revere warning of the approach of the enemy, brandished the testimony of M. King Hubbert, the reports of the Energy Department and Corps of Engineers, and a blizzard of statistics and studies confirming the cause of his alarm, and asked: why no one, in government or out, was doing anything about this real and present danger to our way of life?

It is not just that he did not received an answer. There is no evidence that anyone in a position of responsibility has yet heard the question.

We are Experiencing Technical Difficulties...

Once this shortfall begins, it will not be reversible, for the simple reason that more oil cannot be made. There will be some tinkering around the margins as prices permit the exploitation of more expensive alternative sources, but *science and technology will not be able to change the underlying equation.*

In industrial America, the notion that science and technology are in any way limited, let alone to suggest their inability to meet a challenge that threatens civilization, is tantamount to heresy. Our faith in technology is virtually absolute and a little pathetic. It is reinforced daily in the media, not only in advertising bought by those who profit from technology but in news stories written by uncritical journalists who fail to question their assumptions. Every few hours as this is written, some earnest face over an Exxon logo is assuring us all that with new technology that they are just now deploying, Exxon will lead the way to energy independence.

Congressman Roscoe Bartlett was a well-informed respecter of technology, indeed, he held more than 20 patents for technological inventions. But he was also clear-eyed about technology's limits: "We have very good scientists and engineers, and we have used a lot of enhanced oil recovery. We have used discovery techniques, 3-D, seismic and computer modeling to go out and find more oil, and we have drilled more oil wells than all the rest of the world put together. In spite of better discovery, of aggressive pumping of these fields with this enhanced oil recovery, in spite of drilling more oil wells than all the rest of the world put together, and in spite of finding oil in Alaska and the Gulf of Mexico, we today are producing about half as much oil as we produced in 1970." [45]

If we declared energy independence today, and used only American oil, and were able to gain access to all the reserves that are known to exist in this country, and were able to pump and refine it fast enough to meet existing demand (none of these are safe, or even reasonable, assumptions, but let's just accept them for the sake of the example), we would have enough oil to last for 3.4 years. That's the *best-case* scenario: 39 months of independence and then everything stops. These are the facts that underlay the mindless claims by 2008 presidential candidates John McCain and Hillary Clinton, for example, echoed by Mitt Romney in 2012, that if we unleashed the oil companies (remember the chants of "Drill, Baby, Drill?") we would be on the road to energy independence. We Interrupt This Program...

---

45 Speech to the House of Representative, 05/01/2008

Beginning in 2010, Big Oil and its wholly-owned subsidiaries (Congress, for example, along with many universities and media outlets) stopped humming their old favorite, "Drill, Baby, Drill." and began crooning "Don't Worry, Be Happy." According to the new lyric, we had drilled, baby, drilled and now there was plenty of oil and gas in America, and there would continue to be plenty as long as you don't dare tax or regulate Big Oil. You could even hear the backup singers chanting "Energy independence! Energy independence!" "Peak Oil Scare Fades as Shale, Deepwater Wells Gush Crude," gushed *Bloomberg*, with *Forbes* and *The Wall Street Journal* singing harmony. Alas, the song was wrong.

What inspired the new music was not, as you might expect, the discovery of any new oceans of oil anywhere, but the revival of some old technologies that had been too expensive (and too risky) as long as crude oil was selling for less than $100 per barrel. When it exceeded that mark in 2010, Big Oil produced a gusher -- of hype. A new technology called hydraulic fracturing, or fracking (which was actually decades old, but suddenly economical), would unlock clouds of natural gas from such formations as the Marcellus Shale under West Virginia, Pennsylvania and New York; and oceans of oil from the Bakken Shale under North Dakota. Along with oil from Canada's tar sands, and from ever deeper under the ocean floors, we were cleared to burn, baby, burn.

Here's the reality check. The most important thing to remember is that no one discovered any oil or gas in America that we didn't know was there. Instead, increasingly desperate, expensive and dangerous methods were deployed to get at the last remaining drops of combustible petroleum.

- Fracking (blowing underground shale formations apart with high-pressure bursts of water and a witch's brew of toxic chemicals to release trapped oil and gas) brought a temporary boom to North Dakota, Montana, Texas, (oil) Wyoming and Pennsylvania (gas). But the wells were more expensive, less productive, and played out sooner, than anyone expected. Meanwhile the temporary gas glut from 1500 new gas wells dropped prices to just over one-half the $4 per million BTUs the operators of fracking wells needed to turn a profit. By the end of 2012, about half the gas wells had been shut down because they were not making money, and Chesapeake Energy, the biggest player in the Marcellus field, was on the ropes.

- **Tar sands** operations In Alberta, consisting of scooping up planet-sized gobs of oily dirt, washing them with oceans of water and cooking them with all the natural gas they can frack (using almost as much energy as the finished product would yield) was yielding low grade, corrosive crude. Big Oil proposed to build the Keystone XL pipeline, 2000 miles across the US heartland to the Texas Gulf, to refineries whose products are exported overseas. In January, 2012, President Obama refused to grant the permit for the pipeline. Big Oil returned with applications for various segments of the pipeline, and, at least prior to his re-election in 2012, the President began to see the light at the end of the pipe.

- **Offshore drilling** advocates ignored the April 2010 explosion of a rig that polluted the Gulf of Mexico with the largest oil spill in history (so far: 11 felony convictions, $4.5 billion in fines), and continued to swear, with crossed hearts and fingers, that they can go deeper, safer and deliver more oil, faster. In the Arctic Ocean, for example. Shell Oil set out to demonstrate, in 2012, and in rapid succession: lost control of one of its two drilling rigs, which nearly ran aground; failed Coast Guard certification for its spill-response barge; was blocked by sea ice, in a year in which the sea ice extent was the lowest ever; conducted a test of its containment system that was described by government officials as a "complete disaster"; and, after postponing the whole thing, while attempting to get a huge drilling rig out of Alaska before January 1 (to avoid paying state taxes on it) lost the tow in heavy weather and saw the platform wash up on an uninhabited island. So that went pretty well.

Declaring Independence

Until Mitt Romney, political candidates generally contented themselves with saying that it sure would be nice if somehow, someday, we achieved energy independence. To the extent that words still have meanings, the term means that we would produce as much energy as we consume, thus freeing ourselves from dependence on foreigners. It was about all you could say, reasonably, in a country that burns 20 million barrels of oil a day and has produced at most maybe 10 million.

But in conducting the most fact-free political campaign in history outside of North Korea, Mitt Romney was not constrained by reasonableness. He began to promise "American energy independence." He almost always stumbled when he said it, and then amended it to be "North American energy independence." By which he meant that if you assume the recent gains in US production are going to continue into the far future, and that tar sands recovery will not be hampered by shortages of natural gas, water, investment money, demand or pipelines, and that Mexico's production stops dropping like a severed elevator, which it has been doing since 1980, and steadies out, then -- and only then -- is there a shadow of a chance of anything like independence. (By the way. How is it that dependence on Canada and Mexico somehow translates into independence?)

This could, and should, have been dismissed as another fanciful puff from the Romney smoke machine. But the idea suddenly gained traction when the United States Energy Information Agency and the International Energy Agency (both of which are historically solicitous of the feelings of Big Oil), both reported that the United States was on track to a) pass Saudi Arabia in oil production, and b) achieve energy independence. Headlines and speeches about the US regaining its glory days as world leader in the oil bidness, independent of everyone, began sprouting like pigweed in a field of Monsanto corn.

Couple of problems. One was pointed out by an earlier analysis by the global banking and insurance behemoth Citigroup that found that Saudi Arabia may be *unable to export any oil* by 2030. If the little hairs on the back of your neck did not stand up when you read that, read it again. It says that by the time today's infant is a senior in high school, ten per cent of this country's oil supply will be offline. Permanently. And this Citigroup analysis does not assume any decline in Saudi production, which is highly likely. It simply observes that the skyrocketing demands of the Saudi population will by 2030 be consuming all the oil it can produce. Factor in the likely decline in production (as *Oilprice.com* has done) and the spigot gets turned off in 2022.

What is apparent is that while the US is on track to out-produce Saudi Arabia, it is because the kingdom will be producing less, not because the republic will be producing more. The IEA made the figures look different by changing its definition of "oil."

Another mathematics-based investment bank, Barclay's, looked at the net effect of the much-hyped oil and natural gas "boom" in the United States and estimated it to be, on a scale of one to ten, about zero. Barclay's also looked at the prospects for energy independence as trumpeted by the Romney campaign and estimated the likelihood at — zero.

The numbers, stripped of "plant liquids," NGLs, and other obfuscations, as reported by the US Department of Energy: the US in 2012 produced 6.4 million barrels per day of crude, an increase of 760,000 bpd over 2012. According to ABC News, for example, this represented "an all-time record" and "the highest for any year since 1997." Careful. The all-time record was for the size of the year-to-year *increase*; and while the total was the highest since 1997, it was below every year prior to 1997, going back to about

1953. Just as M. King Hubbert predicted, the United States has never produced more oil than it did in 1970. The year-to-year increases, whether from the Alaska fields or the Bakken shale, are merely bumps on the slide to zero.

While those who profit from oil, and hold office because of oil, and profit from their office, sing mightily the praises of oil now and oil forever; and while we, who can see the mark going lower and lower on the world's dipstick, exhibit the perfect silence of the lambs, who should speak up but a former top official of the much-vilified OPEC, Saadallah Al Fathi. This is what he said::
"Optimism is important for human progress but that does not mean we should ignore what the numbers are telling us."

Chapter Six: Grid Lock

This is a story from our recent past. It's going to happen again, soon.

It begins around noon, on August 14, 2003, in Carmel, Indiana, just north of Indianapolis. The temperature is 86 degrees F., under a mostly clear sky, a little hotter than average for a mid-summer day. But no problems are lighting up the massive, 20-foot by 150-foot monitoring screen in in the control room of the Midwest Independent Transmission System Operator. MISO is the organization that oversees the electrical transmission network for a large chunk of North America -- 15 states and the Canadian province of Manitoba.

Its job is to make sure the enormous system stays balanced. Transmitting electricity is not like routing water through pipes, it's more like herding cats in a thunderstorm. The network delivers electric potential -- voltage -- from electric generators. Turning on an air conditioner draws slightly on that electrical potential; turn on all of the air conditioners in Akron, Ohio, and you can draw it down considerably. When that happens -- and it was happening as the mercury neared 90 degrees F. on August 14 -- the voltage drops at the Akron end of the network, and power instantly flows toward it from all other parts of the network, assuming sufficient generating power is on line to provide it. (If not, and the voltage drop persists, you have a brownout.)

The properties of electricity make managing a grid exceptionally tricky. (There is not one national grid, there are three: one covers the United States and Canada east of the Rocky Mountains, the second handles everything west of the mountains, and then there is one for Texas. The grids comprise 200,000 miles of transmission lines owned by 500 different companies and regulated by the 50 states.)[46]

Thinking of electric current as similar to the pressurized water in your home's pipes does not get you there. You can push water into pipes and leave it there under pressure ready to answer demand. But you cannot store electricity on the grid, you have to manufacture it at precisely the instant it is needed. Electricity travels at nearly the speed of light, so there is no lag time; when you flick the light switch in Philadelphia, the current that answers your call in a nanosecond might come from a hydro-electric dam in Quebec, a coal-burning plant in Ohio or a nuclear generator in South Carolina.

The good news is that you don't have to wait, even a second, for your electricity to be delivered; the down side is that the producers of electricity do not have any time, not even a second, to react to demand, whether it's just you or you and ten thousand of your friends. Electric utilities have to predict maximum demand, and have standby generating power on line ready to answer that demand instantaneously, because if they fall short the result is disastrous – at best a brownout, at worst a blackout.[47]

---

46 Wald, Mathew L., "Wind Energy Bumps into Power Grid's Limits," *The New York Times* August 26, 2008

47 Lerner, Eric J., "What's Wrong With the Grid," *The Industrial Physicist* Vol. IX Issue 5 p. 8

Another complication is the way electricity travels. It does not care about the shortest distance, it follows the path of least electrical resistance, over a network of a myriad of transmission lines whose electric properties change from second to second. There is no way to know, either in advance or afterward, how your electricity gets from point A to point B. Increased demand instantaneously changes the load on all the generators in the network, and on all the transmission lines that link the generators and the demand.

If the system gets out of balance, because of unmet demand or unused supply, the amount of electricity rocketing around the system at the speed of light can exceed the ability of available transmission lines to carry it, causing the lines to heat, or circuit breakers to trip. Sudden demand placed on a generator without the capacity to meet it causes a circuit breaker to shut the generator down before it destroys itself. That creates a sudden, additional drop in the pressure of the network, causing electricity to flow in that direction from elsewhere. These flows, added to the already large demand, could trip out more generators, or could overload more transmission lines. Another consideration is the frequency at which the electric current alternates -- 60 cycles per second, or Hertz. If the current generated into the network is any greater than demand, the frequency starts to climb; if demand exceeds supply the frequency drops. Any change from the required 60 Hertz and a generator will start to heat up and quickly destroy itself unless a circuit breaker takes it off line.

With all this to watch for, along 70,000 miles of transmission lines, the people at MISO had to have on their screen a current and complete picture of the loads on, and supplies to, its network. It had to have the ability to instantaneously bring more generators on line, or tap other system's supplies, in response to increased demand or changes in demand patterns. To manage this the MISO had a state-of-the-art network of remote meters and switches reporting conditions to and taking orders from sophisticated computer programs. The computers built a model of the network flows, and displayed it to the human operators, who had to be alert for anything that looked like it was going to go out of parameters. Reliability was the watchword, the mantra, the religion of the ISO. The human attendants of the huge electrical machine were called "reliability coordinators" and "reliability analysts."

At 12:15 pm. on August 14, a minor glitch in the incoming telemetry drove haywire a critical part of the computer modeling program, called the state estimator. An alert reliability coordinator quickly corrected the problem. *But he forgot to restart the program.* For the rest of the afternoon, the screens in the control room were not displaying some essential information about the state of the network.

Making Waves

As the summer afternoon heated up and the air conditioners came on, the demand in the Akron and Cleveland areas increased more than usual, lowering the voltage in that part of the network, causing power to surge toward it. All over the system, generators ramped up to meet the demand, quickly approaching their limits, and transmission lines began to heat up under the increased loads. To much of this, the reliability controllers and analysts at MISO were oblivious. For an hour and a half the balance of the system teetered, with no corrective action taken.

The "sink" -- as demand areas are called in the transmission business -- toward which all this current was flowing was the metropolitan area of Cleveland and Akron. Generation and distribution of electricity in the area was handled by Ohio Edison and several other electric utilities owned by First Energy Corporation. First Energy did not have a stellar reputation for things such as maintenance, planning and safety. Its 900 megawatt Davis-Besse nuclear generating plant had been shut down for a year by the Nuclear Regulatory Commission (NRC) following the discovery by inspectors of serious deterioration in the reactor. The NRC imposed some major fines, required extensive repairs and increased its oversight of the plant. First Energy's reputation for diligence would not be improved by the events of August 14

At 1:31 pm., an operator in First Energy's Eastlake, Ohio, generating plant (west of Cleveland on Lake Erie) was making a manual adjustment to the generator's output when it momentarily exceeded system capabilities. A circuit breaker shut the unit down, instantaneously taking off line 600 megawatts of current. Now the grid was seriously out of balance, with large quantities of power flowing toward Cleveland and increasing the stress on lines and generators.[48] As operators in First Energy's control room struggled to deal with the problem, a critical part of their computer system, the alarms processor, went down. By remarkable circumstance -- or by operation of Murphy's Law -- both the MISO and First Energy operators were deprived of critical information about what was happening to their networks. Shortly after 3 pm the events started to come faster and harder.

First Energy was also not very good, it turned out, at keeping the trees cut in the rights-of-way under its transmission lines. At 3:06 pm a 345-kilovolt (kV) transmission line south of Cleveland, which had been heating and sagging and heating some more, touched a tree and shorted out. Two more lines, both 345-kV, followed suit within 30 minutes. First Energy controllers got no alarms, and did not know it had happened.[49]

While MISO and First Energy controllers tried to figure out why their networks were mysteriously becoming unstable, they failed to inform system controllers in nearby states that problems were developing. This was a critical sin of omission, not to mention a violation of regulations..

The loss of transmission lines increased the loading on the system in the Akron and Cleveland areas. Between 3:39 and 4:08

48 *Final Report on the August 14, 2003 Blackout in the United States and Canada: Causes and Recommendations* -- US-Canada Power System Outage Task Force PT 11 p. 5
49 *Final Report: On the August 14, 2003 Blackout* New York Independent System Operator February 2005 p 11

pm there was a rapid cascading failure of sixteen 138-kV transmission lines, which shifted load so dramatically that two main 345-kV lines went out, and two breakers between First Energy's network and American Electric Power's tripped under the onslaught of current surging in from the south. In a remarkable telephone conversation reported later in the *New York Times*, a First Energy operator told a counterpart at MISO at this time that the voltage on a major line was dangerously low. "Do you have any idea on what is going on?" MISO replied that the line apparently had been tripped, adding, "I am wondering if it is still out."

"We have no clue," First Energy replied. "Our computer is giving us fits too. We don't even know the status of some of the stuff around us."

MISO agreed: "I can't get the big picture of what's going on. Strange things are all happening at the same time."

The system was now beyond being out of balance. It was collapsing, and the only question that remained was how far outward the effects were going to ripple. By 4:05 pm the voltage swings increased in size to 100 megawatts, tripped the remaining connections between First Energy and American Power, which sent a 2,000 megawatt ripple through the MISO system, knocking off another 900 megawatts of generation. In a 2-second period, five major 345-kV transmission lines in Michigan tripped off line.

Now an enormous tidal wave of power, estimated later to be about 4,000 megawatts in size, surged into the network of the New York Independent System Operator. This was the first indication the New York operators had that anything was amiss, so completely had the Midwestern operators failed to grasp, and to communicate, the size of the unfolding disaster. New York was immediately and totally overwhelmed. The electrical tsunami blew out transmission lines, generators and network interconnects until 50 million people in eight American states including New York City and two Canadian provinces were without power. In all, more than 290 generators were off line, and 34,000 miles of transmission line were out of service.[50]

It took two days to get the power back on, and two years to figure out exactly what had happened. What had happened, essentially, was deregulation.

Deregulation Infatuation

In the beginning, electricity was not thought of as a commodity; it was a necessity of life and commerce, like water and sewer facilities, and as such was regarded as a public utility. That meant that either the government itself provided electricity, or it closely regulated the private companies that did so. The electric companies were granted monopolies in their areas, and in return for being freed from competition in selling something everyone had to have, were required to keep their profits modest. State governments watched over their electric utilities, making sure they built enough generators but not too many, making sure they maintained them and kept them and their operators safe, seeing to it that the rate of return rewarded investors without gouging consumers.

The electrical system that grew under this traditional arrangement was, by and large, satisfactory. Electric utilities, whether privately or publicly owned, were vertically integrated, owning everything from the massive generators at one end of the system, through the transmission lines and distribution systems to the little meter on the house at the other end. Of course people complained about their electric bills, and about the occasional power outage after a storm, that is what people do about bills and inconveniences. Of course the gigantic and wealthy companies that owned utilities gained over time too much influence with the regulatory agencies and politicians, but they were at least restrained by the certainty that wretched excess would bring public outrage and regulatory retribution. Regulated utilities provided

---

50 *Blackout of 2003: Description and Responses* Dennis Ray, Power Systems Engineering Research Center November 5, 2003, slide 8.

cheap electricity to a prosperous and growing nation (not to mention substantial and secure dividends to the nation's investors) for half a century. That began to change with deregulation.

The Reagan Revolution was conducted by industrialists for industrialists, and it consisted of convincing the American people that government was their enemy, the "free market" their friend. Corporations existed only to "create jobs," this new mantra went, and any taxation or regulation of corporations destroyed jobs and increased costs for the little guy. Deregulate, get government out of the way of the rich and powerful, the story went, make them richer and more powerful, and benefits would "trickle down" to the poor and the powerless. The selling of this gibberish to the American middle class, convincing blue-collar Americans that these predators were their friends, is one of history's largest, longest and most successful con jobs. For the CEOs, it was not enough to industrialize almost every human activity, maximizing the profits from every product, they now wanted all restraints short of criminal law removed from commerce. They paid for it, and they got it. On taking office, the Reaganites deregulated everything they could reach, with uniformly disastrous results.

You may object to attributing the deregulation of the electric utilities to the Reagan Revolution on the grounds that President Reagan was long gone from office before it happened, and Bill Clinton was the first president to propose it, albeit unsuccessfully. To argue thus is to seriously underestimate the Reagan Revolution. The case outlined above was sold so massively by the Reaganites that it thoroughly intimidated an entire generation of Democrats. Clinton campaigned, for example, to end "welfare as we know it," and "the era of big government." He did not win office by opposing the Reagan Revolution, but by co-opting it. And he certainly did not pay for his campaign by insulting his major contributors.

It is also fair to point out that the beginning point of deregulation, the first crack in the dominance by regulated monopolies of the electric-utility business, was created by the Carter administration. It was the Public Utility Regulatory Policy Act (PURPA) of 1978 that first ordered public utilities to buy power from independent producers. Like most achievements of government, it had a completely unintended consequence. The intent was to support the development of renewable sources of energy -- wind, solar, micro-hydro and the like -- by forcing the utilities to buy the current generated by small, independent producers. The effect was to set precedents for overriding state regulation and for separating the production of electricity from its delivery. Still, it took nearly 20 years for the industrialists to get the traction to begin seriously to dismantle a system that had been working well for most people.

Why fix what was not broken? The idea was sold to the public as a change that would benefit the ordinary consumer. Simply introduce the benefits of free-market competition into this monopoly-ridden business, the argument went, and electricity suppliers would bid fiercely against each other to keep their rates low and win the business of homeowners and businesses. A leading proponent of this argument in the 1990s -- appearing on its behalf before Congress and state legislatures all over the country -- was an as-yet little-known company called Enron.

Logic wept in the face of the arguments made for deregulation. Why would companies that enjoyed a monopoly and a guaranteed profit voluntarily – hell, eagerly -- subject themselves to rate competition that could only benefit their customers? How much competition could there be when there was, and could be, only one electric line to each house? When the capital costs of getting into the business were so high that only a few companies in the world could afford to get in? With demand increasing daily while any increase in supply took 20 years to accomplish? But companies such as Enron were learning that you could make any argument stick, no matter how silly, if you had the money to put it on enough bumper stickers and in enough 30-second TV spots.

Of course the real motivation behind the selling of deregulation was greed. By the 1990s many electric utilities, especially in California, were suffering from the costs of bringing on line nuclear power plants whose construction and operating costs seemed always to exceed predictions by wide margins. Electric utilities were also affected by the dot-com bubble -- the first of a series of financial gyrations that would lead eventually to the global financial meltdown of 2008. So much money fled the sedate world of regulated-utility returns for the heady promise of double-digit dot-com paybacks, (guaranteed!) that the utilities were having trouble raising capital. Moreover, companies such as Enron, which was not a utility nor did it intend to become one, had dilated nostrils at the scent of the profits to be made if they could just convert electricity to a commodity. [51]

Lavish donations to political candidates of all parties, and relentless promotion of the bogus benefits of the free market, inexorably wore down the resistance of common sense. By legislation (the Energy Policy Act of 1992) and regulation (Orders 888 and 2000 of the Federal Energy Regulatory Commission, or FERC) the federal government pried open the doors to independent electricity producers and pried loose the fingers of state control over them. By the late 1990s, 24 states and the District of Columbia had begun to deregulate their electricity markets. Among the first to complete the process was the largest, California.

It is hard to overstate the toxicity of the gospel of deregulation, of let-the-market decide, as it has been draped over enormous corporations providing the necessities of life (including health care, medicines and health insurance, but that's another story). Giving this gospel free rein in the field of electricity was an immediate bonanza for the wealthy and powerful and an immediate disaster for ordinary people. But at that, the grave

---

51 Slocum, Tyson "Electric Utility Deregulation and the Myths of the Energy Crisis," *Bulletin of Science, Technology & Society*, Vol. 21, No. 6, Dec. 2001 p.2

problems it created in the short term paled in comparison with the long-term dangers of its denial of basic laws of economics and physics. We will return to these larger threats after we consider the prompt collapse of California's electricity supply that should have -- but did not -- put a permanent end to the gospel of deregulation.

California Reaming

California's massive deregulation legislation, written by the utilities and hustled through the state legislature in three weeks, included a $28 billion bailout that compensated the companies for their nuclear-generator boondoggle, on the flimsy ground that since they were regulated when they made the mistakes, they should not be burdened by the consequences in the new competitive age. In exchange for the cash, the utilities agreed to a five-year cap on the price of electricity to consumers -- not at the existing rates, but at 50% above the national average. Outraged California consumers organized an initiative by referendum that would have returned the burden of the utilities' errors to the owners. Consumer organizations spent a million dollars promoting the initiative, the utility companies spent $30 million dollars to oppose it. It lost.

California electric utilities celebrated their escape from monopoly by investing the bailout cash in out-of-state companies having nothing to do with electricity, and in buying back their own stock to put more profits in fewer hands. To raise even more cash to play with, they sold their power plants.

There was another reason for doing this. All regulation of electric utilities rested on the 1935 Federal Power Act, which permitted the state to regulate only the retail price of electricity to consumers. When the sellers of electricity owned the generators, the generators were regulated, and the regulators did not permit divestiture. After deregulation, the retailers remained under some restrictions; as mentioned, California and other state imposed a temporary cap on rates as a trade off for the massive bailout payments. So the utilities sold their generating plants for premium prices, often two or three times book value, to companies happy to pay because their future profits would not be under anyone's control.

Now, instead of a single, vertically integrated company making, transmitting and selling the electricity within its area of monopoly, California had several kinds of entities in the business. There were operators of generators, who could set their rates without regulation, and the old utility companies who now bought electricity at wholesale and sold it at retail. They dealt with each other through a new creature, something called an Independent System Operator. These organizations were created by FERC in 1998 and charged with managing electricity in large multi-state chunks of the country, matching supply with demand and keeping the lights on. Into this mix soon stepped a weird new hybrid, a kind of company that did not make anything, or provide any service, but merely bought and sold contracts for electricity, and the rights to buy contracts in the future, and derivatives of contracts, and so on.

It was the era of supply-side, trickle-down economics, and deregulation was a bonanza on the supply side -- for the companies that generated the electricity and were wheeling and dealing in electricity. (In this context, "wheeling" has a special and pernicious meaning to which we shall return.) According to a Public Citizen analysis of the eight major power companies controlling the supply of California's electricity, from 1999 to 2000 their after tax profit jumped from $3.2 billion to $5.8 billion. One of these companies was Enron, whose story not only embodied the entire, greed-crazed feeding frenzy of electricity deregulation, but foreshadowed the remarkably similar meltdown of the global financial system eight years later.

Both bubbles, the California electricity bubble of the 1990s and the mortgage bubble of the 2000s, were inflated by the fetid breath of derivatives, which blew and blew until the bubble exploded. Enron, not content to buy electricity low and sell high, began to buy contracts for future delivery at a low price and then worked to drive up future prices. Beginning in 1998, investor-owned utilities, appropriately known by their acronym as IOUs, had to buy electricity on a spot market, as if they were playing the stock market. And that is exactly what Enron, among others, was doing. Schemes to manipulate the market became standard operating procedure and were given cute nicknames such as "Ping-Pong," "Death Star" and "Get Shorty." Telephones couldn't handle the volume of deals so they went on the Internet, increasing their trade volume by orders of magnitude. After-tax profit was not good enough so they went to offshore banks and foreign-based "special purpose entities" whose anonymity permitted evasion of both taxes and the consequences of bad bets. Electricity wasn't enough; soon Enron was dealing in things such as Internet bandwidth, lumber and on-line movies.

The bubble inflated wondrously. Enron became the largest energy trader in the world, soon controlling a quarter of all existing electricity and natural-gas contracts. Its stock price tripled in two years, reaching $90 in August of 2000, a year in which it claimed sales of more than $100 billion and reached seventh place on the Fortune 500 list of top companies. In the 1999 presidential campaign it donated $2.3 million dollars, according to the Center for Responsive Politics, most of it going to George W. Bush and the Republican Party. At the outset of the Bush Administration, Enron CEO Kenneth Lay sat down alone with Vice President Cheney to discuss the future energy policies of the United States.

Over on the demand side, things weren't going so well. The old utility companies that were selling electricity to consumers could not raise their retail prices, even after wholesale prices (thanks to Enron and company) skyrocketed. The utilities had happily accepted price caps to get the bailout cash, but had spent all the cash on other things and by 2000 were having great difficulty paying their bills. A drought in the summer of 2000 affected the supply of hydro-electric power from the Pacific Northwest, on which California supplies had become dependent.

There was never an actual shortage of power, but Enron soon discovered that in periods of peak demand all it had to do was take a power plant down for "maintenance" and the prices on the spot market skyrocketed.

As such people do, Enron overplayed its hand. A major heat wave struck California that summer, and manipulated shortages led to massive blackouts, while rising costs, which the utilities could not pass on, led to bankruptcies. Electricity that the regulated companies had produced for three cents per kilowatt hour was now, thanks to the "free market," costing them as much as 50 cents and more -- and they were not permitted to charge their customers more than 6.7 cents. Human parasites seem unable to learn the lesson nature has taught all other kinds of parasite -- never kill your host. Even when winter came and demand slacked off, when the readily available supply of electricity was roughly four times demand, Enron continued to fake shortages, even causing rolling blackouts, to keep prices up.

In January of 2001, with the major California utilities in or near bankruptcy, the state stepped in to buy electricity. Before long it was spending $60 million per day with Enron and a handful of other price-gougers to provide its citizens with a necessity of life. As the state's debt mounted into the tens of billions of dollars, appeals mounted for the federal government to step in. In September of 2001, the federal government imposed price controls on the entire Western electricity market. Spot-market wholesale prices immediately dropped 80%, the rolling blackouts stopped, and within weeks Enron filed for bankruptcy, to be shredded by a myriad of civil lawsuits and criminal charges.

Wheeling and Dealing

Both of the events just described -- the blackout of 2003 and the Enron collapse of 2001 -- were the subjects of extensive news coverage at the time and prolonged discussion afterward (although the Enron case was overshadowed by the events of September 11, 2001). As the country counted the toll of the Enron fiasco -- people had died in manipulated blackouts, the state of California had nearly been bankrupted, companies by the scores, along with employees and investors by the tens of thousands, had been wiped out -- there were heartfelt vows of "never again" and lusty calls for regulatory reform. All of which were forgotten in time for the same thing to happen again on a much larger scale in the housing bubble that ate the economy just five years later.

Likewise after the blackout there were calls for more oversight, better tree-trimming, improved procedures and so on. Virtually none of it happened, and all of it was beside the point.

Here is the vital point -- the moral, if you will -- of both stories. When you try to treat electricity as a commodity, to be bought cheap and sold dear over vast, often trans-continental distances, you not only invite, you mandate, disaster. By the laws of physics, electricity does not travel well, and as we have seen, violations of nature's laws have consequences.

In the beginning, grids consisted of the transmission lines needed to get from a generating plant to the plant's customers. The network was compact and the distances relatively short -- across a city or a handful of counties. The company that owned it was required by regulators to maintain enough reserve generating capacity to meet peak demand, and to explain and justify any changes in its operations, whether they involved taking plants off line for maintenance, or scheduling tree-trimming in rights-of-way or increasing rates. The continuous growth of cities, suburbs and industries that followed World War II challenged the utilities to keep up, and no government entity ever thought seriously about restricting the growth. As a result, utility companies constantly flirted with disaster as they tried to raise capital to increase their generating capacity while managing their networks to maintain reliability.

The electricity industry is not a good place to find examples of economy of scale. It's a wasteful business at best; more than half of the energy contained in the fuels it uses for generation --

coal, natural gas, and uranium -- is wasted as heat. As much as seven per cent of the current produced is lost from transmission lines in normal operations. But when you are laboring under the delusions that your fuel supply is inexhaustible, and your product is so cheap that waste is not noticeable, and your toxic pollution is carried somewhere else by the wind and the water, you carry on.

What was unleashed by deregulation that made the Enron frauds possible and the Northeast blackout inevitable was a practice called wheeling. When electricity was commodotized, and the generating companies were freed of regulation, and daily "spot" markets for buying and selling voltage were established, and the Enronites were intent on buying low and selling high, they started to buy cheap power, hydro from the Pacific Northwest for example, and "wheel" it -- or transmit it across networks, along hundreds of miles of transmission lines, in order to sell it where it would bring more money, for example in southern California. Some of this had been done previously, to meet emergencies, but now it was a daily practice. (It was authorized by FERC's Order 888 in 1996, but delayed by litigation until the Supreme Court approved it in 2000.)[52] Wheeling was what made Enron a lot of its money, the resulting congestion on transmission lines (whether actual or pretended) drove prices up even further and led to blackouts. It was the long-distance wheeling of power that overheated the lines and led to the massive blackout of 2003. In the words of Loren Toole, a transmission-system analyst at Los Alamos National Laboratory, "The system was never designed to handle long-distance wheeling."

One reason that long-distance wheeling is such a problem involves something called reactive power. This is getting a little deep into the territory of physicists and engineers, but in brief, reactive power is current that is generated in such a way that it is 90 degrees out of phase with the alternations of the line voltage.

---

52 Lerner, Eric J., "What's Wrong with the Electric Grid?"*The Industrial Physicist* Vol. 9 Issue 5 p 8

Reactive power is needed to maintain the precise voltage required, and the longer the distance of transmission the more the need for fine-tuning the voltage. One problem is that reactive power does not travel as far as the power it is regulating. Another is that the generating companies that produce reactive power cannot charge for it, and reactive-power production reduces the amount of deliverable power produced. Transmission companies, under the new rules, cannot require generating companies to produce enough reactive power to stabilize voltages and increase system stability.

These days, the industrialists who are muscling in to the renewable-energy industry are proposing to put up massive wind farms on the ridges of West Virginia and the plains of Texas, and enormous solar collectors in the deserts of the southwest, and plug their output into the grid so it can be wheeled to where it is needed, or more accurately, to where it can be sold for the highest profit. They propose all this under the green flag of environmentalism, but there is nothing sustainable about manufacturing and transporting and erecting these wind behemoths with 100-foot blades, or about manufacturing, transporting, constructing and servicing hundreds of acres of solar collectors in an arid and fragile ecosystem, or about the hundreds of miles of new transmission lines that will be required just to connect these sources to a grid, never mind what must be done to increase the capacity of the existing grids to permit the additional wheeling that is presumed by these plans. The Maple Ridge wind farm in upstate New York-- 200 massive wind turbines erected at a cost of $320 million--often cannot deliver its abundant power to customers because the grid is already congested. [53]

In describing one such project -- the Sunrise Powerlink, a proposed system of wind turbines in California's Imperial Valley, feeding a 123-mile transmission line to San Diego -- the *Washington Post* observed that "The nation's richest resources of

---

53 *ibid;* "Wind Energy Bumps Into Power Grid's Limits," *The New York Times* Aug. 26, 2008

renewable fuel -- primarily wind and solar -- lie in distant deserts, vast plains, and remote valleys and hilltops ... far from the populous cities where energy is most needed. Thousands of miles of new power lines will be required to bring renewable energy to cities and suburbs, a vast undertaking that will cost untold billions of dollars in public and private money and will require compromise by dueling interest groups and people ..." [54]

The industrial mindset has become so entrenched in our thinking that those sentences seem to us not only to make sense, but to be the only possible way to frame the problem. But is it really true that the sun only shines on the desert, and the wind only blows on the plains? That the "richest resources" are found in one place, the consumers are in another place, and without industry to connect them we are all lost? Thus framed, the problem has only one solution: build more power plants, a bigger grid, longer transmission lines and continue to ignore the fact that we are running out of the resources we are wasting. Even if we use wind and sunlight to originate current, there is nothing renewable about the steel, copper, aluminum, concrete and other finite resources required by massive transmission lines.

Solar power, as embraced by the industrialists, is even more ridiculous. They (and their ever-compliant Congress, as expressed in the Energy Policy Act of 2005) want to build enormous solar installations in the Mojave Desert, for example, that will use curved mirrors to concentrate the sun's heat on a pipe carrying fluid that will boil water to run a steam turbine. What this process needs in enormous quantities – twice as much as any coal- or gas-fired plant the same size – is water. Water to boil, of course, and then water to cool the whole system, in the hot, arid desert. (As it is, the electricity required by an average household, generated in the traditional way, consumes *three times* the water used by the household for all other purposes. Add to the debit side the water

---

54 "Alternative Energy Still Facing Headwinds," *The Washington Post* February 17, 2009

needed by all the construction and operating people, the damage done to the delicate desert ecosystem, the destructive path of the transmission line to wherever, and you have a prescription for disaster. As of March, 2009, the federal Bureau of Land Management had 158 applications for solar plants that would cover more than a million acres of desert.

Already the "smartest guys in the room" (as the definitive book on the Enron mess derisively called its executives) are the guys setting up the big wind and sun projects. The guys who used to murmur about getting into dot-coms, or Enron, or collectivized debt obligations, are steering clients to "renewables." Technology, we are assured, will solve the problems of electricity distribution, and we will have a "smart grid," a term that gives the back of its hand to the grid we have now. Presumably the "smart grid" will have a way to deal with the dumb operator who neglects to start the software.

Thinking Outside the Grid

The industrial generation and transmission of electric power to hundreds of millions of (primarily urban) consumers has never been, and never will be, sustainable. Something that is not sustainable cannot continue. At some point, the lights are going to go out.

As with oil, the serious problems will start not when we run out, but when we run short. Over the next few decades we can expect our electrical system to become prohibitively expensive, then to experience ever more frequent interruptions of service. Whatever lipstick is applied to this pig, the grid will still consist of wires on sticks, and will continue to be vulnerable to ice, snow, wind, falling trees, sagging lines, excess demand, cascading failure, human error and, above all, greed. However "smart" it becomes, it will remain primarily a stupid way to distribute electricity generated by burning coal and "natural" gas, with all the associated problems of pollution and waste, until the fuel runs out or the grid breaks down.

If you don't believe it can happen to a modern industrialized society, consider South Africa, whose economy is the largest on the continent. After ignoring years of warning about the increasing vulnerability of its electrical system, the entire country experienced sudden, massive blackouts in January of 2008. The country's diamond and platinum mines, the mainstays of its economy, closed for fear of having miners trapped underground without power for their air supply, lights or elevators. They stayed closed for five days, and lost 22% of their production for that quarter. In the years since, South Africa's supply of electricity has remained unreliable -- daily blackouts of five hours' duration are common -- and the underlying problems of coal shortages, aging infrastructure, and insufficient capacity to meet unrestrained demand have not been addressed. The country is profoundly regretting its Reaganite-like drive, begun in the 1990s, to privatize and deregulate what had been a successful and reliable system.

As daunting as are the challenges to, and as bleak as are the prospects of, all the industrialized power systems, it is remarkable to realize that cheap, renewable, sustainable electricity is available right now to anyone who wants it. The problem that cannot be solved for everyone is already solved when you turn it on its head and ask not how can we provide power to everybody, but rather, how can I provide power to my home or business?

To be sustainable, electricity has be generated where it is used. You and I can do that. If our site has lots of sun, we go with solar; if it's gusty, up with a wind turbine; if there's a creek outside the door, we use hydro; if we have a forest we burn wood. We have to evaluate our site and its resources, and we have to design our structure, we can't just slap up another McMansion without regard for where south is, or where the windows are or what the energy budget is going to be. And we have to understand that our motivation for making these choices and incurring this expense is not to save a few pennies per kilowatt hour while continuing to enjoy the life of an energy hog, but to survive when the grid goes dead.

The only "smart" grid is one that does not exist.

PART IV: INSTITUTIONS

"Today we have involved ourselves in a colossal muddle, having blundered in the control of a delicate machine, the working of which we do not understand."

John Maynard Keynes

Chapter Seven: The Failed State

My education in the economics of politics was completed by a ten-minute conversation in the spring of 1995. I had been by then an active student of the subject for 35 years, both as a journalist and an activist. I had participated in political campaigns since 1960, and had managed my first -- for a candidate for the Virginia General Assembly -- in 1965. As a consultant I had engineered an upset victory for a candidate for mayor of Akron, Ohio, and had (albeit briefly because of his early withdrawal) managed three states for the presidential campaign of Senator Howard Baker.

But I still had a lot to learn about the role of money in politics. I had run for the Virginia Senate in 1991, as a kamikaze independent environmentalist in a conservative Republican district. I knew I didn't have a chance of winning but was determined to try to start a public and political discussion of the accelerating deterioration of the environment. I knew, of course, that I could not expect much in the way of campaign donations from the people who shared my views in opposing residential sprawl and industrial pollution -- such people didn't have any extra money -- but they had enthusiasm, and some organization, and at the time I still believed it was possible to beat dollars with votes.

I was explaining my strategy one evening to a potential supporter, a wealthy landowner from the Middleburg Hunt Country, who wanted to know how I was going to deal with the fact that my well-connected opponent would have all kinds of campaign money donated by builders, developers and polluters. I told him that I would make a virtue of my lack of money, and would tag my opponent with being a tool of the special interests. My interviewer had been around the track a few times, and was familiar with the sprawling Senate district and its several cities. "Yeah, well" he responded, politely as always, "It takes a good deal of money to establish poverty."

He was right of course. I did not have enough money to explain to any significant number of people in the district why I was poor, and my opponent rich, or why I was right and my opponent wrong. In the event, of course, I was buried under an avalanche of my opponent's direct mail pieces and radio ads, which had little to do with him or the issues but got lots of repetition.

So I was encouraged, four years later, to receive the nomination of the Democratic Party to run for the same senate seat, and looked forward to a subsequent meeting with the party's long-time top fund raiser and rainmaker. The prospect of benefiting from his legendary ability to produce cash was exhilarating to me, because I believed that if I could campaign on a level playing field and thoroughly communicate my views, I could win. Since I had met with him and other party leaders to explain my approach before getting their nod for the nomination, I was confident that he would help me. The good feelings were short lived.

"Now, I don't have any money of my own," he said as soon as I was seated in his office. (A casual visitor, looking around the cramped office in a seedy shopping center in an industrial part of town, might buy that line, not knowing about his multiple businesses and directorships, his palatial home and wealthy colleagues.) "But I have friends who have money, and they like to support candidates." Good. I waited for their names, and the amounts they would be forwarding to my campaign account.

"Now, here's the thing. They know me, so when I bring a candidate to them, they usually ask only one question." He named the state's giant electric-utility holding company. "Now they will want to know where you stand on permitting new power plants and transmission lines." He named a giant West Virginia coal-mining conglomerate. "They'll ask if you're on board with emission controls." Then there was the humongous homebuilding company with headquarters somewhere in suburban Washington D.C., which would inquire as to my enthusiasm for suburban sprawl.

There were a few more examples, every one of which named companies that were not based in, and did not have significant operations in, the senate district I was seeking to represent. "You see the problem," said the rainmaker. "You just don't have the right answers." I left with his good wishes, and later received from him a personal donation of fifty bucks. In the event, the godfather's friends gave their money to my opponent, who gave them his total loyalty during his long subsequent political career.

This is the nature of the beast that has destroyed the American experiment in government. It is not the overt, coarse corruption depicted in movies and novels, it does not usually involve votes traded for envelopes stuffed with cash, or deals made in coded telephone calls. It is polite and understated for good reason: everyone in the game knows the rules and has no reason to explain or debate, any more than players in a baseball game would stop the action to discuss the subtleties of the designated-hitter rule. In my case, large corporations having little or nothing to do with the district or its people exercised decisive influence over the choice of the area's representatives.

Our system of representative democracy was designed expressly to prevent this, to assure that ordinary people -- including the poor and the powerless -- have direct access to and influence over their representatives. This clause of the social contract says that so long as you, the office-holder, pay attention to me, the voter, you will get my vote and stay in office. What the Money has done is disconnect this link. Pay attention to me and my needs, the Money says, and I will give you enough cash to buy your office, and all you have to do stay there is keep me happy and keep your constituents from getting so angry that they rediscover the importance and the power of the vote.

I did not give up after my disappointing session with the party godfather. I contacted a professional fund raiser who, after sizing up my balance sheet and prospects on the phone, reluctantly agreed to meet with me. He flew his private plane into an airport in the district and at a brief meeting there laid down the conditions under which he would agree to work for me. I would have to commit to spending a minimum of six hours per day, six days a week, on the telephone, calling everyone and anyone I had ever met in my life to ask them for money. And if I wanted to get re-elected, he said, that would be how I would have to spend my four-year term of office.

This is what people in the game knew and I did not, what all the political pundits and writers and movies and books on politics pretend is not the case: that the daily work of a politician (at any level above county commissioner or town council) does not consist of reading, thinking or talking about policies, legislation, government or the welfare of people. It consists mainly of raising money -- begging for it on the phone and in person, attending fund raising events, and going to meetings to make plans for fund raising. The average cost of a campaign for the US House of Representatives is well north of one million dollars, and for the US Senate, a minimum would be three million dollars. That means that a member of Congress must raise an average of *at least* $10,000 every week -- $2,000 per business day -- in order to have any expectation of re-election.

Imagine getting up every day of your life knowing that on that day you had to convince someone to give you at least $2,000. A great many people these days affect a glib cynicism about politicians that I do not share. I have worked closely with scores of candidates and officeholders in my life, have known scores more, and the vast majority of them were honorable people dedicated to public service. Of course there was no golden age of virtue in the game, in my lifetime or anyone else's, during which no one used public life to grasp for money, sex and/or power. The illness that overtook politics and government in this country in my lifetime was not the changing character of the participants but the changing nature of the process. To explain, I need to go into more detail about politics as I found it 40 years ago.

Someone who wished to rise in politics then faced a triad of tests. The first required taking an active role in the affairs of the party, performing menial tasks, participating in party activities and meetings, long enough to come to the favorable attention of the party's leaders. The second requirement was a demonstration to the financial backers of the party, who were not the same people as the tactical leaders, of readiness, willingness and ability to represent their interests. Then, with a nomination and funding within reach, one had to show a talent for connecting with the public and winning votes. The strength of this system was in its diversity. Like a three-legged stool, it worked best when its three parts, each requiring a different skill set, were well balanced.

Partisanship was a different animal then. One chose a party in much the same way one chose a football team to support. Often, one simply continued a family tradition. (I once asked a lifelong and highly effective politician why he had joined a party other than his family's traditional favorite. After long, hard thought, he answered: "The people seemed nicer.") One bought the tickets, cheered the victories, booed the opponents and remained loyal without much concern for ideology. It's true, you can look it up: the Republican Party had its liberals -- Mayor John Lindsay of New York and Vice President Nelson Rockefeller, for example -- in addition to its Barry Goldwaters; and Democrats had a southern contingent that in some respects dwelled to the right of Goldwater. The parties were teams, and just teams, loose organizations that competed in elections but had little role in government and no deeper meaning. Of course we talked trash about the other side, which of course accused us of all kinds of malfeasance and misfeasance, but it was in the manner of football fans who shriek insults during the game but afterward are still friends. I remember the Democratic and Republican candidates for the General Assembly of Virginia car-pooling to debates -- riding home together! -- something that has been inconceivable for more than two decades of campaigns characterized by vicious idealogical and personal attacks.

Campaign management was different, too. The process by which votes were assembled was largely retail, which is to say it was based on personal appeals by the candidate to small groups of people. The function of a campaign organization, an experienced consultant once told me, was to nail down votes one at a time until you had 50 per cent plus one. A candidate started his morning greeting workers at a factory gate, went to a few gatherings over coffee, canvassed door-to-door in mid-morning, spoke at a luncheon meeting, canvassed in the afternoon, spoke at a dinner and perhaps another event in the evening. Management consisted of targeting the candidate's activities -- using vote histories and demographic information to make them as effective as possible -- while spreading his influence with phone banks, surrogates and advertising.

Candidates came to the public square with ideas and policies tested in their own lives. As quaint as it may seem now, when I became active in politics candidates did not consult polls or focus groups to find out what it was safe to say; they said what they believed and waited for the judgment of election day. Most people I knew then thought it repugnant even to consider packaging and advertising a candidate "like a brand of soap," as it was usually put. Even at that, long before the advent of take-no-prisoners politics, there were people who were uncomfortable just with the necessity of calling attention to themselves.

One of the most honorable such men I ever knew was J. Kenneth Robinson, a Shenandoah Valley orchardist who in the 1970s and 80s served in the state Senate and in the US Congress. He hated campaigning -- making speeches, holding news conferences, traveling and eating rubber chicken in front of gawkers made him excruciatingly uncomfortable. He relished studying issues and discussing them with his peers, but every two years as he approached the three-month campaign (yes, that's how long it was then; it started officially on Labor Day) he declared that it would be his last. Late in his career I asked him why it was that he vowed to quit every two years but ended up running again. Teasing, I asked him if it was the perks of the office, the fame, or the big bucks. He gave me a baleful look. "No," he said, using an extremely rare epithet, "It's the sons of bitches who want to succeed me." This was not partisan or personal rancor; he saw the people who were after his seat as overly ambitious, self-centered and greedy, while at the same time insufficiently informed and motivated to do the job.

Of course there were in those days such things as greed, and blind ambition, and corruption. But the system was diverse, diversity made it onto the ballots, and diversity often kept the cancers in check. Men like Kenneth Robinson were, in my early experience, far more numerous than, for example, those such as his colleague Wilbur Mills, the Arkansas congressmen who became famous for his drunken escapades with the stripper Fanne Foxe.

The role of money was different then. Candidates were, then as now, usually wealthier than the rest of us, for several reasons. Most political offices below the rank of governor or member of Congress were part-time jobs with little pay; you had to be financially secure enough to be able to take substantial time away from your occupation and to make do with the skimpy remuneration. State legislatures, like the Congress, were set up originally to be convenient for farmers, who could deliberate at length during the winter months without sacrifice of personal income. As I came to know politics in the 1960s, it was most frequently lawyers who had freedom to arrange their schedules and incomes so that they could pursue significant offices. As for the financial demands of the campaign, you had to have cash for buttons and ads and direct mail, but raising it was no more difficult than any other challenge of running for office.

Hard to believe today, but consider: John C. Stennis went to the United States Senate from Mississippi in 1947 and stayed there for more than 40 years. In all that time, until 1982, he never spent more than $5,000 in a statewide re-election campaign. But that year, as part of the Reagan Revolution that had captured the Presidency and the Senate majority, a man on fire named Haley Barbour came after Stennis with hammer, tongs and a big advertising budget. The first campaign consultant Senator Stennis had ever engaged, Raymond D. Strother, told him he would need to raise $2 million to keep his seat. The courtly senator, 80 years old at the time, had no idea where to get that kind of money.

"In desperation," Strother recalled, "I reminded the old senator that he was chairman of [the] Armed Services [Committee] and had spent billions of dollars with the defense industry. What about LTV? I asked him. What about McDonnell Douglas?"
"Would that be proper?" he asked.

Strother, who did as much as anyone to usher in the era of modern, money-centric, no-holds-barred politics, wrote 20 years later that the question still haunted him:

"Is it proper for a public official to take money from companies and institutions over which he or she holds great power? Is it proper for state treasurers to collect campaign money from banks? Is it proper that fund raising must start for the reelection campaign the day after the election? Who gets first call on a public official's time, the person who votes and writes a note or the person who raises $100,000? The answers are obvious and an insult to democracy.

"Long before the Senate tied itself in knots over the McCain-Feingold campaign finance reform bill in 2001, Senator Stennis had put his finger on something that none of the reformers in modern politics wanted to touch: It is not only bad form to take money from industries regulated by Congress, it's an inherent conflict of interest. What Congress has done over the years is to practically legalize bribery.

"Days later, after our conversation about fund raising, Senator Stennis called me over to his office. He said he had a surprise. He reached into his desk drawer and handed me a check from LTV. I was astonished. It was for $100. But he was proud and I didn't have the heart to explain. His honor would not allow him to beg. Later, other senators did the dirty work for him and raised more than a million dollars for his campaign."[55]

Stennis won, served six more years, and then left the Senate standing up, with his financial integrity intact.

The Rise of the Moneycrats

Trends and events can be easily and glibly packaged in neat decade-sized packets with short labels. Understanding them is

[55] Strother, Raymond D., "Falling Up: How a Redneck Helped Invent Political Consulting," remarks given at the Festival of the Book, Charlottesville Virginia March 20, 2003.

much more difficult. But for all the clichés that are spouted about the 1960s, there can be little doubt that with their assassinations of cherished leaders, the prosecution of a brutal and unpopular war in Vietnam with its associated student demonstrations and riots, the decade marked a turning point for our country, and not a positive one. The wellsprings of many trends can be found in those turbulent years, but let us observe a mantra of the 1970s and follow the Money.

Let's be clear about what I mean by the [capitalized] Money. If I referred to (Roman) Catholics, I would have in mind the whole church, in a general way -- its leaders, its dogma, its members. By the Money I mean the cardinals and practitioners of the Church of the Currency, the religion that dominates the culture of this country and much of the world. It is the consensus of our society that money is the measure of everything. We are defined by the amount of money we have, and the amount of money other people have calibrates our attitude toward them, the degree to which we are dismissive or obsequious. Only in such a society could the Trickle-Down school of economics -- which says that if we give the rich free rein to get richer, some benefit will trickle down to the rest of us -- be greeted by anything other than ridicule. We act, communally, as if the possession of money, whether by accident, criminality, inheritance, lottery or work, confers intelligence, happiness and superiority. We act and talk this way in the face of an infinity of evidence that nothing could be further from the truth, and despite the dictum of the nominal religion to which most of us pretend to subscribe, that the love of money is the root of all evil.

If you are running for office, you had better have more money than your opponent if you expect to be taken seriously, no matter how inspired your plan to reform health care. If you are running a company, you had better report more income this quarter than last, no matter how comfortable your profit margin was last quarter. If you do not have money, you must have it; and if you do

166

have money, you must have more. Thus has the Golden Rule by which we live become: Whoever has the Gold, Rules.

The rise of the influence of money in politics parallels the rise of television. In the 1960 presidential campaign, John Kennedy "won" his debate with Richard Nixon on television – Nixon had a five o'clock shadow, appeared to be sweating, and seemed to many people to look, well, shifty. Most people who listened to the debate on radio, on the other hand, thought Nixon won because he sounded crisp and knowledgeable. Thereafter, attention had to be paid to how a politician looked and to how he handled himself on this new medium. Television advertising -- as opposed to coverage -- came to the fore in the 1964 campaign, during which Lyndon Johnson's campaign prepared an ad showing a sweet little "Daisy Girl" being incinerated by a nuclear weapon, thus indirectly raising the question of whether Johnson's opponent Barry Goldwater would, if elected, precipitate nuclear war.

This landmark in the descent of American politics deserves further examination.

- The ad ran only a few times, but was given saturation exposure, for free, by news programs that ran it while discussing the controversy it ignited.
- The ad made no argument, and used no logic. Indeed, it made only three statements: these are the stakes; we must love each other or die; vote for Lyndon Johnson.
- You could comprehend the argument embedded in the ad only if you knew that candidate Goldwater had expressed a willingness to use "tactical" nuclear weapons on the battlefield, just a few years after the Cuban Missile Crisis had brought a terrified world face to face with the prospect of nuclear annihilation.
- Since the ad made no argument, it could not be refuted. Goldwater supporters could only complain that it was somehow wrong to frighten people with the prospect of nuclear war, somehow underhanded to suggest Goldwater

was unstable. The Johnson people shrugged, and went on to a landslide victory. (By stating those two things in close proximity – they ran the ad, they won the election -- I do not mean to imply that one thing caused the other. But you see how it's done.)

The lesson -- that you do not have to make sense to win an election -- was not lost on the people who would shortly engineer the Reagan Revolution and more.

Would You Repeat That?

A few years later I had a small personal experience that drove the point home in a way I would never forget. I was a broadcast newscaster, and part of my daily routine was reviewing the stack of news releases that each mail delivery brought. Every week, the local USO sent a schedule of its entertainment for service members, which I scanned for anything out of the ordinary. Every time I saw it, the schedule noted the Friday night appearance of a singer I'll call Bonnie Blue.

One day, an acquaintance called. His organization was planning a coffee-house event and wondered if I knew of an entertainer they might engage. "You might try Bonnie Blue," I said at once, "I hear she's pretty good."

It wasn't until I had hung up that I realized what I had said. I called him back right away. "I didn't mean to mislead you," I said, "but I have no idea who Bonnie Blue is or what kind of an entertainer she is. All I know is that the USO books her every week. She might for all I know be the talent-starved daughter of the USO club manager." I never got over the ease with which I had been suckered, however unintentionally. The simple repetition of a name, without even any attached adjectives, had led me to associate positive qualities with that name.

The rise of television (in 1942 there were about 5,000 TV sets in the country; 20 years later more than 90% of all American homes had one) and of America's addiction to it, provided a powerful medium with which to sell products and ideas by simple repetition; all that was needed to make an enormous number of people fall in love with a product or a person was cash. For the politician, TV changed all the equations. Now, instead of thinking through policy and legislation, and honing debating skills, one had to think up slogans and jingles. To be competitive, political thought had to be expressed in 30 seconds. To be effective, the 30-second argument had to be repeated endlessly, which took enormous amounts of money, which was available of course only from those who had it. House Speaker Tip O'Neill used to say that money was the mother's milk of politics; with the advent of TV it became the oxygen.

With so much money required for an advertising campaign, candidates began to protect their investments in the same way the marketers of soap did, by research. They used polls to find out what people were thinking, and then announced that they agreed. They used focus panels to gauge peoples' reaction to being told what they already thought, and honed their messages accordingly. The days when one related the lessons one had learned, outlined some new ideas for governance, and took one's chances, were over.

Television conveyed another benefit to the Money and its now-wholly-owned politicians. It functioned as a powerful narcotic, a "one-eyed god," as someone has said, "that every night turns millions to stone." People on couches, sedated by an endless stream of sitcoms and murder-mysteries, do not attend city council meetings. People accustomed to bumper-sticker political philosophy and cartoon digestive systems and the bright hysterical world of advertising images do not ask complex questions, or require long answers. It is well-established opinion that any population in the world, no matter how advanced or prosperous, is just three missed meals away from rising in revolution; what, you have to wonder, would be the effect on the American population of three days without any television?

As powerful as TV was, it was still possible to reach a tipping point at which the maximization of profit at the expense of human misery, for example in the prosecution of a pointless war, made enough people mad enough, or afraid enough, to forsake their diversions, take to the streets and remember that enough remained of democracy to assure that motivated votes could still beat millions of dollars. This happened in the late 1960s, toward the end of the Vietnam War, when those afraid of the military draft and those appalled by the seemingly endless war made common cause and ended any number of political careers including that of President Lyndon Johnson. It happened again in the 1970s, when the callous criminality of the Nixon administration became so obnoxious that he was driven from office.

The Money learned that the two best ways to prevent such uprisings were diversion and division; providing public sideshows that either distracted most people from what was going on, or portraying events in such a way as to divide opinion evenly, pro and con. Certain issues became evergreen for their ability to divert and divide at the same time: abortion, flag-burning, gun rights and gay rights, for example. But in this regard, nothing was better than an enemy. And godless Communism was a near-perfect enemy; distant, different not only in political philosophy but religion and to a certain extent ethnicity, well enough armed to be realistically scary and manipulative enough that great powers and vast plots could credibly be attributed to it. For 40 years it served as the organizing principle of national American politics, an ideal enemy and distraction. Richard Nixon made his political bones as an anti-communist running against people he labeled as "pink." It was never a question of whether you were for or against Communism, it was a question of whether you were "tough" enough on it, a quality demonstrated by the shrillness of your invective against it and you willingness to fund any weapons system or initiative that could conceivably be used against it.

Another useful diversion was partisanship. In the 1980s, as politicians found they needed more and more money to gain political power, and as their service to the sources of that money became necessarily more and more blatant, they found it useful to make partisanship more ideological. It was as if one football team and its fans came to believe that passing was the only kind of play that was legitimate, and began to revile any team or player that ran with the ball, while other teams with equal fervor refused to pass, executed only running plays, and expressed hatred for those who threw the ball. In this way the political parties began to claim that certain styles of governing and thinking were legitimate while others were not, with regard only to their ideology and not to their efficacy. Republicans began to profess the belief that tax cuts and less government regulation were the solution to any problem, any time, any place; and Democrats proposed new laws and new government programs for every conceivable ill.

Ideological partisanship made bumper-sticker, sound-bite politics easier because once you drank the Kool-Aid of your party you knew what you thought about any question before you heard the question. Reviling your ideological enemies made fund-raising easier because there is nothing like fear and anger to get someone to empty his head and his pockets on your behalf. It is tempting to say that this is what changed politics, that ideological partisanship ruined the country. But it was not the cause, it was one of the effects of what really happened -- the rise of the insatiable need for cash for the candidates, and of ways to distract the constituents from what their representatives were doing to get the cash.

All these needs were met in the Reagan Revolution that came to fruition in 1980. The man who was not a president but could play one on TV put an amiable face on an ugly agenda that was anti-Communist, anti-government, anti-tax, anti-social-security and anti- "welfare queen" while ignoring the rapidly worsening problems of massive pollution, unbridled development, profligate waste of natural resources, increasing dependence on dwindling supplies of oil, and mounting threats to supplies of water and food. His predecessor, Jimmy Carter, had desperately tried to focus the country on the need to address its addiction to

171

foreign oil, but even after two stunning interruptions in supply had brought the country briefly to one knee, his efforts earned only ridicule from the sunny actor who defeated him. Government was not part of the solution, Reagan said over and over again, it was the problem. He thus denied the original, fundamental reason for the institution of governments: to protect the powerless from the strong, and did it so charmingly that the powerless bought his argument.

By masterfully manipulating public fears and anger with lavish campaign spending, Reagan's handlers not only got him elected, but re-elected. It did not seem to matter that while vowing to cut the size of government he increased it; that while promising to reduce federal spending he increased it, sinking the country into debt of historic size; that while saying he would reduce everyone's taxes he did so mainly for the rich, whose tax rates went from 70% to under 30%, while most working people saw their payroll taxes increase. None of it seemed to matter at the polls. He and his "conservative" movement convinced the middle class, especially the less educated blue-collar workers, that service to wealthy industrialists was in their best interests. It was one of the largest and most successful con jobs of all history.

Until it was surpassed by the advent of George W. Bush and his "architect," political consultant Karl Rove. Rove distilled the dark arts of political manipulation in service to the Money to a degree of toxicity never before seen. Among the maxims that set him astride the political world for a decade:

- Leadership was accomplished not by unifying people in support of a compelling vision, but by dividing people into ideologically armed camps and then appealing to your camp, or "base," making them so frightened and angry that they will vote in greater numbers than their opponents' camps.

- If you spent enough money repeating *anything*, people would believe it, as long as an equal amount of money was not spent simultaneously in denying it. Their artistry was at its best, or worst, when they achieved a 70% majority of the American public who believed that Iraq was involved in the terrorist attacks of 9/11; and they did this without ever saying it was so, they just meticulously placed the two words -- Iraq and 9/11 -- in close proximity every time they addressed the subject.

- As a corollary of the point above, when threatened by an opponent it was not necessary to spend time and money trying to find his weaknesses, you simply attacked his strength. Thus when Bush, widely regarded as a draft-shirker, was faced by John Kerry, a decorated and wounded war hero, the tactic was to deny, belittle and mock his heroism. The tactic did not require facts, only repetition. Its execution and success in this campaign contributed a new word to the language – the verb Swift-boating. The Bush machine used the same tactic on John McCain (accused during a primary contest in 2004 of having been unbalanced by his years of torture as a prisoner of war, and of fathering a black baby out of wedlock, presumably a reference to an Asian child he and his wife adopted) and Georgia Senator Max Cleland (a triple amputee as a result of wounds suffered in Viet Nam, defeated after groundless claims he faked heroism after being injured in an accident).

Let's call it industrial politics. Like industrial farming, industrial politics has transformed a process that was intended to enhance the security and well-being of people into one that erodes both; has converted public service into service of the powerful, without regard for collateral damage. Just as small farms were once diverse interlocking systems capable of sustaining themselves, so politics served well when it did not let one part of its triad – loyalty to the party, service to the money or popularity with the voters -- exceed any other in importance. Industrial politics, like industrial agriculture, is committed to monoculture: its only crop is cash.

In the years that it has been tightening its grip on the American political system, the Money has sold, in addition to any number of bad policies and bad people, a noxious set of principles that an unsuspecting public has largely adopted as part of the American Way of Life.

Not content with the unhealthy respect for money already embedded in the society, or with the ability conveyed by having unlimited cash with which to buy unlimited media, the Money has relentlessly associated money with speech. On its face this makes no sense, but endless repetition has made it seem familiar and acceptable. Its effect is to drape with the mantle of one of our most precious freedoms – the freedom of speech – the practice of subverting government to the service of Money. It's a small change, really, from guaranteeing the freedom of an ordinary person to speak his mind without fear, to guaranteeing that a corporation or billionaire can without limitation use his wealth to flood the commercial airwaves with a point of view, drowning out the views of the less rich. Instead of guaranteeing the right to speak, we are in this case guaranteeing the right to be heard. It is as if our Constitution guaranteed to the rich not the pursuit of happiness, but its attainment.

In January of 2010, the Supreme Court of the United States ruled, in the landmark case *Citizens United v Federal Election Commission,* that corporations hold First Amendment (freedom of speech) rights under the Constitution to spend freely to support or oppose candidates for federal office. As it happened the case did not concern the prohibition of corporate funding of political candidates and parties, but although the decision left that prohibition standing, it was chain-sawed halfway through at the base and swaying in a high wind..

As a corollary to the equating of money and speech, the

174

manipulators have succeeded to an unfortunate degree in equating corporations and persons. The claim is necessary if you are going to seek protection under the Constitution. One cannot, obviously, grant the freedom of speech to a rock, or a machine. Thus we are told that corporations are really citizens, and have the same rights to participate in politics as any "one" else. (The HBO series "True Blood," in 2008, offered a similar and equally sensible argument, portraying a future in which vampires, despite being, um, dead, and despite their need to drink human blood, were given the same societal rights and protections as other "people.") Corporations resemble people about as much as sharks do. Corporations are created for one purpose, to make money. They spend their entire lives ingesting money, and are judged by no other standard.

What the Money has done to and with our political system, the people and the policies it has advanced by defeating votes with dollars, is bad enough. What is worse, and is doing even more to bring down this country, is what the Money has prevented government from doing. Especially since the 1980s, as we have seen, the Money has pulled the regulatory teeth and claws of government in any area where there is money to be made, from oil to housing development, from genetically manipulating corn to financially manipulating derivatives markets.

As the horizons have darkened with the gathering clouds of mortal threats to our food, water, oil, electricity and health, not one single agency of government, nor one credible national leader, has proposed effective measures of response. Not one. Nothing effective has been proposed to mitigate, let alone avert, global climate change. Nothing has been suggested that would ease the effects of peak oil, of eroding soil or worsening water shortages in the West and South.

Indeed, during the protracted presidential and congressional elections campaigns of 2012, the only mentions made of the various existential threats to our way of life were denials. We were treated to the spectacle of platoons of candidates for Leader of the

Free World (or so Americans like to think of their president) testifying that they did not believe in climate change, evolution, taxes or regulating polluters.

Much of this feigned ignorance was in response to the threat of the Tea Party, whose rise and fall during the first term of Barack Obama has been misunderstood. Appearing suddenly in 2009, a few months after Obama's inauguration, it was widely identified by pundits as a populist uprising, a spontaneous combustion of people oppressed by taxation, regulation and government debt. In reality, it was about as spontaneous as a symphony orchestra, an uprising of oppressed people who had a bankroll of at least $12 million for buses, signs, ads, walking-around money and the other necessities of populism.

The money came primarily from David and Charles Koch, of Koch Industries, the second-largest privately held company in the United States. Second-generation billionaires and long-time funders of right-wing causes and candidates, the Kochs had been dismayed by Obama's victory in 2008 and were determined that it not be repeated. Their Tea Party became expert at whipping up enough neurotic anger about "socialism" and taxes and regulation to defeat more reasonable conservatives in GOP primaries. So much so that the fear of being "primaried" became the dominant concern of virtually all candidates for public office in 2010. Tea Party candidates did well in the Congressional elections of 2010, and fear of them persisted into the runup to 2012.

It was in many respects the ugliest election cycle in living memory. Blizzards of vicious attack ads, a great many of them paid for by the corporations unleashed by the *Citizens United* decision, savaged candidates on any grounds that could be imagined, without regard for truth, or for consequences for lying. When the candidates got a chance to speak for themselves, they pandered shamelessly, promising to manage the economy, create jobs, lower taxes, find oil, whatever we wanted. But curtail the ravages of industry? Protect the helpless from impending shortages of food, water, transportation and energy? Didn't come up.

It was as if the passengers on the *Titanic,* as it sailed full speed into a sea of icebergs, contemplated electing a new captain based on the color of his uniform and his promises to serve more caviar at the all-you-can-eat banquets. Danger to the ship of state? What danger?

And yet it must be noted that the ugliest tactics, backed by the most money, mostly failed. The hundreds of millions of dollars spent by the Kochs, plus the hundreds of millions marshaled by GOP strategist Karl Rove, Las Vegas casino owner Sheldon Adelson and others made it the priciest presidential election ever; something between five and six billion dollars was spent. Yet the Money lost. It not only failed to unseat Obama, but lost the great majority of the Congressional candidates it backed.

And that is encouraging. But the people who won still have to raise a gazillion dollars a day to keep their offices, and to get it they have to go to people just like the Koch Brothers and Sheldon Adelson, people who have money to give away and who want something for it.

Thus the lockdown continues, and while the oceans rise and the storms get worse and the West burns and the Midwest blows away and the wells go dry and the mark on the nation's dipstick gets ever lower, tomorrow's candidates will continue to argue about gay rights, the debt ceiling, voter fraud and other diversions. Government of the Money, by the Money, for the Money shall not perish anytime soon.

Chapter Eight: Running with Banks

The economic crisis that began in 2008 provided a template for the coming collapse of the other industrialized systems – such as those that now provide our food, water and energy -- whose only purpose has become to make more money, faster. The events also demonstrated that a government in service to financial interests rather than its people cannot, in a crisis, protect anyone, even the very financial interests that command their loyalty. Consider the similarities between the financial system, as it was in, say, early 2005, and the food, water and energy systems as they are today:

- Enormous cash profits engendered not only wealth, but a sense of entitlement and infallibility in the Masters of the Universe who were making unimaginable fortunes. Moreover, the money inspired admiration, if not awe, on the part of the public, the journalists who are supposed to inform the public, and the regulators and legislators who are supposed to protect the public.

- To the extent that they had accumulated cash, the players and institutions had become influential in politics, achieving – especially after 1980 – the deregulation that allowed them to set up a casino economy in which they played with OPM – Other Peoples' Money.

- Illogical propositions were repeated endlessly until they became familiar and accepted. Experts announced that they had suspended the laws of logic and nature, and no one laughed. At the height of the casino economy, the so-called investment banks were hiring mathematicians to write equations that supposedly quantified risk but that turned out to be merely an uptown version of what a drunk tells his wife after losing their savings at the race track. A Texas hedge-fund manager who saw disaster coming long before the crash, Kyle Bass, talked to the New York rating agencies who were using sophisticated computer programs to evaluate the risks of investing in complex derivatives based on pools of mortgages. He told the CNBC program "House of Cards" that the algorithms all assumed that housing would appreciate between 6% and 8% per year -- *forever.* No one contemplated the possibility of a future decline in housing prices. Other occupations not yet in ruins continued to operate after the meltdown on the basis of equally silly notions -- that the yields of monoculture crops will increase forever, for example, or that a finite resource such as fresh water or oil can be used with abandon forever.

- Public discussion of the practices and their consequences was conducted with bumper-sticker slogans and twisted words whose meaning had been corrupted. It was a "sub-prime mortgage crisis" that could be "contained," not an endemic failure of a global system based on unsustainable levels of debt, consumption and waste. At the bumper-sticker level of discourse, it sounded reasonable to say that we were going to "kick-start" the economy by borrowing money from China to give to banks so they would lend more money to consumers. But the economy broke down because consumers were buying luxuries they could not afford, with money borrowed against future income and their perpetually appreciating houses. When the time came that they could not borrow any more on their houses, or with their credit cards, and were facing unemployment, the question became: how do you kick-start a dead horse?

- There were journalists who tried to examine the processes in play, to suggest their logical and inevitable consequences, and to explain what happened after it happened. But for the most part, corporate journalism remained focused on the search for higher ratings (or circulation) and profit margins, which it thought it could achieve with simplistic explanations and over-hyped conflict. Apparently convinced that its audience was afflicted with attention-deficit disorder, industrial journalism forgot that it cannot exist except among a free people, and that its primary duty is to give people the information they need to stay free. Even – or especially – when that information is complicated, or unwelcome.

In order to understand both what happened, and what it portends for the rest of our world, we need to review the record.

The Way it Was

As with all history, the meaning of this narrative depends on where you begin it. The year in which the unwinding of the modern financial world began was 1980. But as we take up that story, let's remember a more distant time, when people worked and saved for years before acquiring a house, when a mortgage was a mark of shame, when debt was unsavory and usury was a crime.

The shared values that people expressed, not only in their conversation but more importantly in the way they lived their lives, included high regard for productive work, a satisfaction derived from living within one's means, and deep suspicion of conspicuous consumption. This is not meant to be a description of a Golden Age in which greed and corruption did not exist, but rather a fair summary of the cultural norms of the United States for at least two decades after the Great Depression.

It is very difficult for most of us to imagine now, let alone remember, a time when living life seldom involved borrowing money. I happened to be present at a small turning point in this life when in the 1960s I knew a furniture dealer in Bermuda who introduced to that sleepy, behind-the-times colony the concept of consumer credit, or as the British called it, hire-purchase. He allowed people to take possession of furniture with a small down payment and a contract to pay the remainder with interest to a finance company that he also owned. Within a short time, he told me with some amazement, he was making more money from the finance company than he was from the furniture company. His innovation was greeted on the island with indignation, especially on the part of his competitors, but also quite genuinely on the part of people who believed that unearned possessions, like unearned wealth, corroded the character.

The reservation seems quaint in a time and among people who value nothing so much as unearned wealth – lottery winnings, inheritance, CEO compensation and the like – and unearned possessions acquired by credit card, or with nothing down. Just as we value money more than anything, we are valued above all as consumers. (The President of the United States, addressing the nation after the terrorist attacks of 9/11 2001, about to embark on what he would call the Global War on Terrorism, urged his fellow citizens to demonstrate their faith in the cause by going shopping.) Delaying gratification – saving earned money for a car, a house or an engagement ring – has been transformed from a prime indicator of maturity to the earmark of a loser. On the other end of the equation, that of the producers, the realization of my friend in the furniture business that he could make more money by moving money around than by selling things, was the gasoline that set the world afire.

The Fire Last Time

The observation that the recession of 2008 and forward was the worst since the Great Depression has become a cliché. It is well to remember that the Depression was brought on in part by greed and corruption in the banks. It was common, before the crash, for a bank to invest its money in a company's stock, then lend the company their depositors' money, then encourage their depositors to buy more of the stock. As long as everything went well, there was no problem with all this circular dealing. But when companies started to fail, banks rushed in with other peoples' money to try to prop up their deteriorating position. But you cannot prop up a building that has started to fall, and before long the whole thing – the banking system of the entire country – collapsed. It is argued that it was not the self-dealing that brought the banks down, but rather the decline in property values triggered by the Depression. That is like arguing that it is not the fall from the skyscraper that kills you, it is the sudden stop – it's a distinction without a difference. As we learned again in 2008, any financial feeding frenzy that depends on the perpetual, uninterrupted appreciation of assets is doomed.

In reaction to the role played by financiers in causing the Depression, Congress passed the Glass-Steagall Act, as the Banking Act of 1933 became known. The legislation addressed the primary evil of pre-Depression banking – the conflict of interests that exists when a company makes part of its profit by keeping your money safe, and makes the rest of its profit by gambling with the very same money. The Act separated guardianship from gambling by prohibiting banks from owning or dealing in securities, and prohibiting brokerage companies from accepting deposits for safekeeping. To prevent ruinous competition for deposits among banks, its Regulation Q limited the amount of interest banks could offer on savings accounts, and prohibited the paying of any interest on checking accounts. To restore confidence in the banking system, it created the Federal Deposit Insurance Corporation to protect depositors' accounts in the event of bank failure. In the 1950s the Act was extended to prevent banks from underwriting insurance; they could sell insurance products but they were not to assume the risk themselves.

The assumption was that there was a public interest – which is to say a government interest – in making sure that people had access to a safe place to put their money. This was not possible, the evidence of the 1920s and 1930s attested, in the absence of laws preventing bankers from taking the money in the front door and running with it out the back door to the nearest casino – whether that be a futures market, a derivatives market or a plain old stock market. For the next forty-seven years, as economist Paul Krugman put it, banking was boring. Limited to the function of protecting its depositors' money by, for example, lending it only to those who could pay it back, and investing it in only the safest of instruments, the profession was not well paid and not especially attractive to the criminal mind. During those five decades the bank owners continually did everything they could think of to get around, over or under Glass-Steagall, or to get it repealed. But the public interest in the safety of deposits held firm until the Reagan Revolution sold the slogan that government was not the solution, but the problem. In 1980, Glass-Steagall was repealed and the advent of another depression was thus assured.

The first step was passage of legislation (the Depository Institutions Deregulation and Monetary Control Act of 1980) that disposed of the crime of usury by removing the limits on the interest rates banks could offer or charge. This ambivalently named act, the title of which offered both "deregulation" and "control," put the banks under the control of the Federal Reserve, but in so doing took them out from under the regulations of the states, which had been rigorous (it was the states, after all, who had set the usury limits on such things as credit cards and consumer loans). The act unleashed banks to merge, and saving-and-loan associations to offer checking accounts and make commercial and consumer loans -- which is to say to act like banks.

Two years later, the deregulation-maddened Congress further eviscerated the states' control over banking by revoking their mandate that all home mortgages be the plain vanilla variety, with a fixed interest rate, amortizing downward to a zero balance over a stated number of years. The Alternative Mortgage Transaction Parity Act of 1982 opened wide the door to adjustable-rate mortgages (translation: we give you a teaser rate for a year or two, then slam you with a massive increase in payments), balloon-payment mortgages (translation: we entice you with a low payment, then at the end of the term slam you with an impossibly large lump-sum payment) and interest-only mortgages requiring you to pay only the interest for a period of time, making for an even lower teaser payment for the first few years. In 1986 the tax laws were "reformed" to allow people to deduct from their taxable income any and all interest paid for loans on their real estate, but not any other kind of interest expense. Thereafter it made sense to refinance your house to pay off your credit cards because you would both lower the interest rate you had to pay, and make it tax-deductible.

These provisions began immediately to have predictable, indeed inevitable, results. For one thing, loan originators started giving mortgages to people who previously would not have qualified because of their income. With more people in the market with more spending power, housing prices began to climb After four decades of boredom, banking was interesting again, and attractive to the criminal mind.

There was one other inevitable consequence. Immediately upon being freed from regulations that prevented them from doing stupid things, bankers began doing stupid things. Especially, the bankers who were running the formerly sedate savings-and-loan associations. S&Ls had been even more boring than banks during the 1940s, 50s and 60s, limited as they were to offering savings accounts and mortgage loans. (These limitations, like those on the banks, had been imposed after unrestrained greed brought on a previous, wild crash known as the Panic of 1893. Perhaps we do live in a nation afflicted with Attention Deficit Disorder.) In that splendid middle of the American Century, the S&Ls had been among the many institutions that were regarded – and regarded themselves – as having purposes larger than profit. S&Ls were mostly non-profit mutual associations that were proud of their missions of encouraging thrift (they were even called "thrifts") and home ownership.

Suddenly freed from regulation, the S&Ls went nuts, offering hysterically high interest rates for deposits and making dumb loans to try to recoup their increased expenses until, only five years into the deregulated 80s, they crashed. About half of them, more than a thousand, failed, and cleaning up the wreckage cost the US Government about $160 billion, which in the 1980s was a lot of money.[56] The number of new houses being built each year was cut almost in half, dropping from 1.8 million in 1985 to one million in 1991. The US economy went into recession.

The moment the national economy was again sitting up in bed and taking nourishment, the deregulators, undeterred by the disaster they had brought on, went back into action. In 1994, Congress repealed the laws that had prevented bank holding companies (which enjoyed considerably more freedom from regulation than the banks themselves) from crossing state lines.

As the 1990s progressed, more and more people began to make their living by moving money around, taking a little bit of it every time they moved it. In the boring 1970s and into the 1980s,

---

56 Curry, Timothy and Shinut, Lynn, *The Cost of the Savings and Loan Crisis: Truth and Consequences.* FDIC Banking Review December 2000

the financial sector – those who make their living by moving money – made about 16 per cent of the corporate profits realized in the United States. That doubled in the 1990s, to 30 per cent (and topped 40 per cent shortly after 2000). These people formed a herd that stampeded in the direction of any promise of a rate of return a little higher than the present rate of return. In the mid-1980s they galloped across the countryside dumping cash into any S&L that raised its interest rates a half point above the competitors'. In the mid-1990s the thundering herd dumped piles of cash on anyone who came up with a notion about a way to use the Internet to make money. (My personal favorite memory from this time is of the firm that used its initial-public-offering money, $500 million as I recall it, working on a super-sophisticated marketing program. When they burned up their cash and flamed out, they had a hell of a marketing plan – and NO PRODUCT.) These flows of cash bore a striking resemblance to what happens in the electric grid before it breaks down – great surges of money begin to slosh around the system, overheating everything until circuit-breakers start to pop and take the system down.

The new bubble burst on March 10, 2000, the day the NASDAQ Composite Index, a sampling made up of mostly technology stocks, crested at its all-time high, 5048, and began a two-year decline to near 1000 late in 2002. The fairy-tale, startup dot-coms evaporated (with a handful of exceptions such as Ebay and Amazon) along with their venture capital. The "day-traders," who had left their clerical jobs to sit at their computers all day shuffling stocks in virtual companies, as if snapping down playing cards at a felt-covered poker table, crashed and burned. Five trillion dollars worth of NASDAQ market equity evaporated in the seven months following the peak of its composite index.[57] In the aftermath, formerly venerable companies such as Citigroup and Merrill Lynch were fined millions of dollars for misleading investors about the prospects of the dot-coms. (Yet we were

---

57 "Will The Dot-Com Bubble Burst Again?" *Los Angeles Times,* July 16, 2006

shocked to learn, just a few years later, that the same two formerly venerable firms had been just as unwise, and just as disingenuous, with respect to sub-prime mortgages and their derivatives.) WorldCom filed the second largest bankruptcy in US history after it was exposed for having lied about its profits. A recession ensued.

After the S&L debacle, there had been a pause of nearly a decade while the wreckage was swept up and the thundering herd rested up from its stampede. Not this time. The next bubble was beginning to swell, and the herd was beginning to run in a new direction *before the dot-com bubble had fully collapsed.* The new direction – the Next Big Thing – was housing.

Even mortgage banking had become interesting. Freed from the restraints of decades, whiz kids began to design new "products" among which two would become extraordinarily significant. One would come to be known as the sub-prime mortgage, a name that obscured the reality that these were loans that in all probability would never be repaid. The other would be called mortgage-backed securities, or MBSs, which resembled shares in a company except that the asset was not a company but a pool of mortgages. The second product enabled the first to take off. In the world of boring banking a lender would not approve a candidate who had a poor credit rating or insufficient income to repay the loan, for the simple reason that the lender had to collect the money in order to realize a profit. No more. In the brave new world of deregulated banking, lenders – who were now not bankers but kids working out of storefronts -- collected their profit on the loan, all of it, the minute they got it done and out the door to a consolidator; who, in turn, made his profit the minute he signed up the investors in his mortgage-backed security.

Legislation passed in 1999 (the Gramm-Leach-Bliley Act) repealed most of the tattered remains of the Glass-Steagall Act and unleashed to an even greater degree the same companies whose lack of judgment in the matter of the dot-com bubble were on full display, just a few months before their self-induced collapse. Given near-absolute freedom to do as they pleased, they did what their industry has always done when free – stampeded toward the edge of a cliff.

If you like assigning characteristics to decades, call the one that began in 1998 the Decade of Irrational Exuberance (a term used by Federal Reserve Bank Chairman Alan Greenspan in referring to the dot-com bubble). By 1999, private lenders originated about $160 billion in loans to sub-prime borrowers. This was quadruple the $40 billion that went into such loans in 1994, which in turn was quadruple the $10 billion of such loans made in 1991. All this lending occurred without the participation of the so-called Government Sponsored Enterprises, or GSEs (the Federal National Mortgage Association, known as "Fannie Mae," and the Federal Home Loan Mortgage Corporation, or "Freddie Mac") that previously had been the country's principle buyers of home mortgages from originators, and the leading sellers of mortgage-backed securities.[58] Of these sub-prime loans, only 16 per cent were for the purpose of buying homes; the rest were made to replace existing, smaller loans, with the additional cash used to pay off credit cards, to buy consumer products, or to repair or improve the home.

The feeding frenzy reached its acme in the mid-1990s. Former pizza deliverers who could use laptops were fighting each other to get at anyone with a rambler and a deck of maxed-out credit cards for whom they could "originate" a mortgage, almost always a "re-fi." The flow of money was astonishing. One small-town "broker" I talked to at the time had a list of 20 investors standing by to take any loan she wrote. How long does it usually take, I asked her, after someone pays off their credit cards by refinancing their home, before they return with credit cards maxed out again? Often within 90 days, she said, and occasionally before

---

58 Temkin, Kenneth et al, *Subprime Markets, the Role of GSEs, and Risk-Based Pricing*. US Department of Housing and Urban Development, March 2002.

the paperwork on the first re-fi had fully cleared her office.

When the loan closed, the originator earned her commission, and never saw the loan again. Not for her to worry about whether it got repaid. Collection of the payments was handed off to a processing company while the loan itself was grouped with others to form the basis of some mortgage-backed securities, which sold out as fast as they were issued. Now the individual investors who had funded the loans were bought out, they had their profit and they had their investment back, so they could go out and do it again. The faster, the better.

Thus described, the whole process sounds nuts, which, of course, it was, as was eventually made abundantly clear. But here's what the people inside the frenzy were telling themselves. The companies and individuals writing the sub-prime loans convinced themselves that they were smart enough to find, among all the sub-prime applicants, those whose credit scores were unjustly low, whose reliability had been unfairly impugned, who were better than their statistics indicated. The investors who funded the loans told themselves that the elevated risk of lending to sub-prime candidates was covered by the high interest rates and upfront fees the borrowers had to pay, and the fact that the value of their houses was rapidly increasing – *and always would.* The investors who bought the MBSs told themselves that by pooling the mortgages they had spread the risk – surely not everybody would default – thus diluting it to a degree that was appropriate for the uncommonly high rates of return being offered.

As the game began, these little bits of lipstick applied to a large, growing and increasingly smelly pig made everyone swoon at its beauty. "My God," as the old Cockney song goes, "how the money rolls in." Former burger flippers got rich flipping mortgages; the slightly more ambitious and well-heeled made fortunes flipping houses and condominiums (in 2002, up to 85% of the condominium units sold in Florida were immediately put back on the market and sold by an owner who never moved in, and sometimes never saw it); and virtually every financial institution on the planet sopped up the new currency spawned by this hysteria – the MBSs – as fast as they could be issued. The loan originators ran out of those special, unfairly-branded sub-prime candidates in a few months, after which any candidate would do. Their products became known as "liars' loans" in which the income figure was filled in (often by the loan originator, not the applicant) with whatever number qualified the applicant for the loan, without substantiation; "Ninja" loans, meaning the applicant had "No Income, No Job, No Assets;" Neutron loans, which made the people disappear but left the building unharmed; negative-amortization loans, with payments so low the longer you made payments on it the larger your debt; and so on.

There would be recriminations later about the irresponsibility of the sub-prime borrowers who took out loans without understanding the terms, who signed papers not knowing what was written on them. (The investment bankers who understood neither the terms nor the nature nor the consequences of the derivative crap they were buying and selling would get, right to the end of the game and beyond, multi-million-dollar bonuses.) But the home buyers did not need to understand the long-term deal because they were told, and they had reason to believe, that the minute the payments began to cramp their style, the minute they ran short of cash, they would simply refinance. And so the good times rolled on, on credit. Household debt in the United States was about $705 billion at the end of 1974, which amounted to 60% of Americans' disposable personal income. By the end of 2000, household debt was ten times that, and in 2008 it would reach $14.5 trillion, or 134% of disposable personal income. The entire population of the Unites States was, on average, insolvent.

Occasionally the odor of the sty would waft into the executive suites as someone would look around and, well, wonder. In response to this tiny, occasional quiver of doubt the Masters of the Universe came up with a new, synthetic lipstick: the credit default swap, or CDS. This was an insurance policy against bad debt, which could not be called an insurance policy because to do so would bring it under the purview of government regulation. As with banking, there was a long-standing social contract that said: if huge companies were going to collect premiums from ordinary people on a promise to pay them if their homes burned down or their husbands died or their cars were wrecked, and the companies were going to make substantial money from the practice, the public and their government had a legitimate interest in the companies' ability to make good on their promises. Insurance companies' practices were and still are closely regulated, especially with regard to the reserves maintained with which to meet losses.

No such troublesome details dogged CDSs. If you are owed a debt, and you want reassurance that you will be repaid if something happens to the debtor, you give me some money and I'll give you the assurance. I don't give you any evidence of my ability to pay your eventual claim, and you don't ask for it, because in most cases the guarantee was of a real-estate mortgage, and everyone knew that the value of real estate would increase forever, and no one would ever lose money in real estate. It was, one cynic observed, like taking out an insurance policy on the Titanic – from another passenger on the Titanic.

Another bit of legerdemain made CDSs attractive in another way. When they were issued by, for example, a unit of AIG, the world's biggest and soundest insurance company (although the division of AIG involved in CDSs was not, of course, an insurance company) it came from a company with a triple-A credit rating, the best there is. If you were a bank or an actual insurance company, with investments in mortgage-backed securities that had a bit of an odor about them, your regulators might want you to put more money in reserve against the possibility of default; but not if you brandished synthetic insurance policies from a triple-A rated company! Nobody noticed, until it was far too late, that the rating companies had been bought by, and/or depended for their financial survival on, the companies they were rating. Or that the companies issuing CDSs had accepted obligations far beyond their ability to meet. When the music stopped, the face value of all the CDSs in force was reported to be greater than the value of the entire world's economy.[59]

Thus the frenzy built upon itself. If anyone or any company stopped to say "Wait a minute, this is crazy," other people and other companies, offering sky-high returns to their clients and sky-high volume to their owners, would immediately take the doubter's job, customers, assets and prospects. But credit is good only so long as debts are repaid. In this house of credit cards, the bottom card was the credit extended to those least likely to be able to repay it, and the next card up was the faith that if the borrower defaulted his house would be worth more than it had been when he bought it, could easily be resold, and the creditor thus made whole. Both of these cards fell over in 2005, and the rest of the cards balanced atop them, as this is written four years later, are still falling.

Although the housing market hit the wall in the fall of 2005, few would admit it for another year. Indeed, like the proverbial chicken whose feet don't know its head is gone, even while the prices and numbers of sales of new and existing houses were dropping fast and while loan delinquencies and foreclosures were rising even faster, sub-prime lenders shoveled another $640 billion into the abyss in 2006. Another year later, with the housing pig dead and decomposing in the sty, the still delirious stock market sent the Dow Jones Industrial Average over 14,000 for the first time in its history.

That was July 19, 2007. It was pretty much the last good day for the Masters of the Universe. The fire that had been kindled in 1980, that had been fed and doused and fed again for more than 25 years, on which the Masters had been pouring gasoline since the

---

59 Creadon, Patrick *et al, IOUSA: One Nation. Under Stress. In Debt.*
www.iousathemovie.com

turn of the century, had set the world on fire. Investors around the world began taking a long-deferred second look at the sales pitch that had been used to separate them from billions of dollars, suddenly smelled the decomposing pig, and the whole thundering herd stopped lending each other money. Just like that. All at once the sub-prime-loan originators were marching into bankruptcy like cattle to slaughter: Mortgage Lenders Network USA, Ownit Mortgage Solutions, New Century Financial, American Home Mortgage Investment Corporation and – almost – Countrywide Financial Corporation, the biggest mortgage lender in the country.

Then the sub-prime brush fire crowned, and started taking down the forest's larger trees. Three hedge funds owned by the legendary Bear Stearns Companies exploded, incinerating more than two billion dollars in the blink of an eye. And the fire leapt the oceans and became global, as banks and investment houses all over the world – Switzerland's UBS, Germany's Deutsche Bank, and others in England, Ireland, Iceland, Japan and so on – looked into their vaults and saw, to their horror, smoldering piles of mortgage-backed securities. When they went to get their fire extinguishers – corresponding piles of credit default swaps – the fire extinguishers were on fire too.

In a single weekend in mid-September, 2008, the towers began to come down. The formerly 100-billion-dollar securities fund Merrill Lynch, the largest in the country, on the brink of insolvency because of its exposure to sub-prime derivatives, sold itself to Bank of America for half its value. Bank of America did the deal reluctantly, under intense pressure from the Secretary of the Treasury to do its patriotic duty to avoid a financial meltdown. Which ensued anyway when the same day, another enormous securities firm, Lehman Brothers, went into bankruptcy and dissolution. And AIG, the world's largest insurance firm, pleaded for federal funds because the obligations incurred by one tiny division of the company, that had been selling credit default swaps like counterfeit Rolexes, had brought the entire company within days of insolvency.60

Two of the premises of the bailout and stimulus efforts begun by the Bush Administration in the fall of 2008 and continued by Obama's in the spring of 2009 were 1) that deficit spending was required to lessen the effects of recession; and 2) that certain businesses had become too big to fail without catastrophic collateral damage. These included AIG but not, for some reason, Lehman Brothers. Most people calling for massive programs to "kick-start" the economy cited the Great Depression, and the fact that Roosevelt borrowed and spent heavily, after which the Depression ended.

But caveats are necessary here. The fact that the rooster crowed, and then the sun rose, does not necessarily mean that the rooster raised the sun. Another event that had something to do with the ending of the Depression, was World War II. Moreover, Roosevelt borrowed mostly from Americans (does anybody remember War Bonds?), and the money he borrowed went to pay Americans for American products and services. And when the debts were repaid, most of that money went to Americans, too. Bush and Obama, on the other hand, had to borrow their money mostly from China, to see much of it return immediately to China for consumer goods that we don't make any more, or to foreign banks to retire toxic deals.

The argument that a company is too big to fail reminds me of the principle espoused by the psychiatrist and writer M. Scott Peck (*The Road Less Traveled, People of the Lie*, etc.) that all mental illness begins with an attempt to avoid legitimate suffering. The dry rot that suffuses our institutions today is largely the result of attempts to avoid legitimate pain, to make sure that taxes are never increased, purchases never deferred, discomfort never borne and consequences always for somebody else. It is amazing how quickly the high priests of the Free Enterprise System, who

---

60 "Lehman Files for Bankruptcy; Merrill Is Sold" *The New York Times* 09/15/08

worship individual responsibility when they are making millions of dollars, instantly become socialists when there are losses to be borne. It's even more remarkable how quickly their government follows them in this transformation, until you remember that in the good times, their profits funded the campaigns of countless politicians, so that in the bad times, their government would be there for them. It's just another kind of credit default swap.

The efforts of the Obama administration to bail out, prop up and kick-start the economy, however well meaning, were fated never to achieve the unstated goal assumed by the language used -- to return things to the way they were before. All the credit cards were maxed out, all the assets had been devalued and all the creative paperwork experienced spontaneous combustion. The mortgage flippers and condo flippers went back to flipping burgers, and everyone's expectations experienced dramatic downward revision.

Aftershocks decimated the American automobile industry, twisted the girders of the commercial real estate industry and rattled the windows of the credit card industry. What was clear was that this time there would be no return to normal. The so-called prosperity of the new millennium, during which the rich got filthy rich and the middle class became the lower-middle class, was based on a Ponzi scheme run with borrowed money: consumers borrowed money on their credit cards and their homes to buy stuff from companies; when the companies selling the stuff showed a profit, other companies borrowed money and bought them; investors borrowed money to buy the stock of the profitable companies, while sophisticated investors borrowed money to bet on whether the stocks would go up or down, or to trade in derivatives of derivatives of shares.

In the absence of another massive shock, it seems unlikely that a financial meltdown will lead directly, or soon, to the systemic breakdown that I believe to be inevitable. But it does give us a detailed picture of the mind-set of the people who will take the system down, the inability of government to save us, and the ease and speed with which the unthinkable becomes brutal reality

The Fire Next Time

It would be a mistake to think, after all the dramatics of the recession/depression/ meltdown/ bailout, all of it the "worst since the Great Depression," that we have actually come through anything. When the eye of the hurricane passes over you, the air gets wondrously still, but it would be naive to conclude that the storm is over. In the blink of an eye the wind is blowing just as hard again, from a different direction.

David Walker used to be the Comptroller General of the United States. As the auditor of the nation's finances, he was as close to the numbers, and understood them as well, as anyone. And his hair has been on fire for years, both before and after the recent troubles. "We had a huge structural problem before the [2008] recession, bailouts, all these crises," he says, "and now it's all worse." He was talking about the enormous and rapidly growing national debt, the unrestrained increases in government spending, and the ever-widening trade deficits. Long before the most recent recession began he was touring the country on what he called a "Fiscal Wake-Up Tour," conducting town hall meetings in which he tried to warn the American people face to face about what he called "a fiscal cancer growing within us," which, untreated, could have "catastrophic consequences for our country."

When George W. Bush took office in 2000, the federal debt totaled $5.6 trillion (56% of GDP[61])and was going down. After eight years of cutting taxes and fighting wars, he left behind a debt somewhere north of $10 trillion (70% of GDP). Barack Obama added six trillion dollars to that in the first term of his presidency as he pumped borrowed cash into the ailing economy, in the form

---

61 Gross Domestic Product, a measure of the country's total economic activity.

of bailouts and stimulus programs. It could be said that he reacted to a crisis that had been brought on by deficit spending (by consumers) with massive deficit spending (by the government). There were those who saw this as the equivalent of fighting a fire with gasoline. But Keynesian economists insisted that this is what governments must do to mitigate the effects of economic reverses. When your house is burning down, they insist, it makes no sense to stop fighting the fire because you have exceeded your fire-fighting budget.

But logic tells us that no source of money is infinite. According to the chairman of the Senate Committee on the Budget, Kent Conrad, in 2007 the United States borrowed 65% of all the money borrowed by all the countries in the world, an amount that was 10 times the amount borrowed by the country that came in second. And that was before the bailouts and the stimulus programs began. By 2012 the debt had reached $16 trillion, 102% of GDP.

Those who worry about the fact that all this money must someday be paid back, with interest, are told that there is nothing wrong with deficit spending, that it was deficit spending that got us out of the Great Depression, that the nation's credit is good, and that deficits have not hurt the country in the past, nor have they led to the inflation that was widely and hysterically predicted would follow the deficits of '09 and '10 and '11.

An important reason that deficit spending has not hurt the country before is that in the past, it was indulged in briefly, during times of war or recession, with the debt paid down quickly thereafter. But in the past three decades there have been only five years in which the federal budget was not in deficit. Just as you can pretend the oil will never run out, you can pretend the money will never run out. But it will. At some point, given the continuation of unrestrained borrowing, the Treasury Bill, backed by the full faith and credit of the United States, will become the newest version of the sub prime mortgage. Acording to Peter G. Peterson, a former

Secretary of Commerce, former chairman of the Council on Foreign Relations, and senior chairman of the Blackstone Group, the situation then "will make the current [2008] crisis look like petty cash."

One of the biggest enablers of our addiction to borrowed money has been the Peoples' Republic of China. In 2008, China passed Japan as our lender of first resort. For four years, China held more of our debt (well over a trillion dollars) than any other country. Then China began to experience ecoomic problems of its own, and started scaling back, until early in 2013 Japan was poised to become our biggest lender once again.

(When people contemplate the size of our debt to China, a country with which we have not had the warmest of relations, they draw comfort from the argument that China would never do something rash like refusing to buy our Treasury bonds, or taking their reserves out of the dollar into another currency, because if they did so, and ruined our economy, they would be ruining their best customer. And that is a sound observation to make – today. But the day after tomorrow, when we have passed peak oil, and there is not enough oil to go around, and the survival of industrial countries depends on beating out other industrialized countries for such oil as is available, what will China prefer then? A good customer, or survival?)

Some but not all of the furor over the national debt has been whipped up by the Tea Party since 2009 (when you-know-who was elected president; deficits never seem to bring people into the streets when they are incurred for wars, just when they're used to help people). One wild accusation has trod on the heels of another: China will foreclose and bring us to our knees; the Federal Reserve is printing money to sustain the deficit and will blow up the economy; the Job Creators will leave the country unless we cut their taxes; and on, and on.

The reality is dangerous, but quieter. Of the $16 trillion we owe, only $5.3 trillion is owed overseas; $10.7 is held by US government agencies ($6 trillion), US companies and investors ($3 trillion) and the Fed ($1.7 trillion).

The accumulation and manipulation of public debt, especially when it is used to avoid legitimate suffering, (i.e. the imposition of taxes to buy what we need) is a cancer on the Industrial Age. As we have seen in the collapse of the housing bubble, runaway debt can metastasize, and can kill its host. But the public debt is a slow-acting disease. What the housing bubble triggered was a private matter, and that is where we are truly vulnerable.

The Opposite of Clean and Sober

It has become a cliché to say that we are addicted to foreign oil. But we suffer from a far worse and even more destructive addiction – to money. Let's not just pass over this as a cute expression, like "Jeez, I'm really addicted to potato chips." Let's consider the implications.

> The dictionary definition of **ad·dic·tion:** *The condition of being habitually or compulsively occupied with or or involved in something. In physical addiction, the body adapts to the substance being used and gradually requires increased amounts to reproduce the effects originally produced by smaller doses.*

We -- all of us, in our entire society – are compulsively occupied with money. It was meant to be a medium of exchange, a way of trading work for food, but it has become the standard by which everything is measured. If it makes dollars, it makes sense, we say to each other, as we decide what to do with our lives and our resources. To make money we sacrifice our time, health, families and ethics, and we reserve our most unrestrained admiration for those who have made the most. The recent book

Affluenza[62] defines the illness as "a painful, contagious, socially transmitted condition of overload, debt, anxiety and waste resulting from the dogged pursuit of more."

Most addictions cause shame before the larger society, and encourage their practitioners to conceal their unnatural appetites. But this addiction, being shared by just about everyone, requires display. It is as if the whole world were a crack house, where normal values not only do not exist, but are scorned. The car we drive, the house we live in, the clothes we wear, the brands of things we accumulate – they all serve as badges of the extent of our addiction.

Then there is the second part of that definition: addicts require ever larger doses of the substance they are abusing to reproduce the pleasure, and, eventually, just to keep from feeling sick. There is no such thing in our culture as enough money. Making enough to live comfortably is not sufficient, you must be making more than you did last year. A company making a healthy profit is despised in the marketplace if its profit is not selling more and making more than it was 90 days ago. Is there a choice between using a piece of ground as a park, as a place to reclaim waste water, or as a site for a hundred houses? The highest and best use is the one that generates the most cash.

Like all addictions, like all illnesses, this one eventually, if left untreated, kills.

Of all the evidence pointing toward the inevitability of a crash of our industrial society, nothing is more persuasive than our unwillingness to recognize, let alone treat, this destructive and worsening addiction. Indeed, in the wake of a near-crash of our industrial airplane brought on by pilots overdosing on Big Money, we are not even asking them not to shoot up while the nose of our craft is pointed at the rocks below.

---

62 De Graaf, John; Wann, David; and Naylor, Thomas N., *Affluenza: The All-Consuming Epidemic.* Berrett-Koehler Publishers 2002.

PART V. THE END GAME

"On the last day of the world
I would want to plant a tree."

W.S. Merwyn

Chapter Nine: Apocalypse When?

In our society we are not very good at thinking about risk, let alone catastrophe. We will without a whiff of anxiety strap ourselves into a ton of steel and hurl it down a road at a mile a minute, passing within a few feet of other such missiles at closing speeds of 120 miles per hour (with one or more of the operators likely to be talking on a cell phone or applying makeup) – a practice that every year claims about 50,000 American lives, as many as were killed in the entire Vietnam War. Then we will get an anxiety attack about getting on an airplane, a mode of transport that kills perhaps 200 Americans a year. We worry about what's on our minds, and ignore what isn't. Often we are so focused on trying to start the car that we miss the train that's bearing down on us.

It's a matter of attention, and our culture directs our attention to the things the culture wants us to worry about. The repository of our culture, the holder of our institutional wisdom, used to be the clan or the family, later the church and school. The transmitter of culture used to be the clan chief or shaman or the storyteller, later the teacher and the priest. Their entire motivation was to help us be the best members of the group that we could be, by sharing with us the accumulated wisdom of centuries.

Today we get our culture from the TV set, which has two purposes: to sell us stuff and to distract us from the world. All day and all night, it murmurs to us to worry about gaining weight, losing hair, restless leg syndrome, erectile dysfunction and illegal immigrants. And it tells us what not to worry about: all we need to do to solve the energy crisis is get behind the caring people of Exxon; all we need to know about processed food is that Cargill cares about its customers, and Archer Daniels Midland wants to feed the world's hungry. For the rest of us there's a heartburn remedy you can take *before* you overeat. Now back to murders that never go unsolved (in about an hour), illnesses that never go uncured and sex that never has consequences.

No wonder so many of the things that happen in the real world take us by surprise. We smoke a pack of cigarettes a day for 30 years and start to have trouble breathing. Who knew? We build our house on the river or by the sea because we like the view and one day it washes away. Who knew? Turns out that beautiful forest setting was flammable, and one day the house burns down. Who knew? Answer: everybody knew, but nobody thought about it.

After a disaster we like to tell each other that until the moment it happened such a thing was "unthinkable." We know, of course, that anything can be thought, but we'd rather put it that way than admit to living in denial, to ignoring a threat that we knew, the moment it was realized, was there all along, not only predictable but inevitable.

Members of the George W. Bush Administration were famous for saying that no one could have predicted the devastation of New Orleans by Hurricane Katrina, when the Bush Administration itself had predicted exactly that, and had conducted a major exercise to practice a response. What a hurricane would undoubtedly do to New Orleans was not unthinkable, it was just unthought of, by a lot of people who had responsibility for dealing with the consequences. That includes the people who lived there: an enduring memory of the aftermath was the footage of a resident standing in swirling flood water, bellowing to the camera: "What are we supposed to do?"

We are all good at ignoring unpleasant prospects. We know, for example, that one day in the foreseeable future we are going to die. That expectation could easily overshadow everything that happens to us while we're waiting, but we hardly ever think about it. Note, however, that the folks who have an economic interest in our passing, for example the purveyors of life insurance, funerals and cemetery lots, have ways of draping the unthinkable with euphemisms that allow us to buy their stuff while keeping our eyes averted from what the stuff is for. "If something happens," don't you want insurance to make your family so rich they won't miss you? "At time of need," wouldn't it be a good idea to have a paid-up contract with the undertaker? And how about the view from the cemetery plot? You're going to love it there.

Confront any reasonable person with, for example, the logical realities of the world's oil supply (as described in Chapter Five) and he will acknowledge that in the near future he, personally, is going to have to live with much less oil. Direct his attention to his life as a commuter, shopper, importer of his daily food from thousands of miles away, and he will acknowledge that without massive changes in his life there is no way he can make the transition – that he and his family are exposed to terrible risk. Leave the room, and he will stop thinking about it.

Just as nothing is unthinkable, so nothing is incredible, which is to say incapable of being believed. A significant number of Americans, around 20 per cent in many polls, believe in extra-terrestrial abductions, or in a living Elvis, or that President Obama is a secret Muslim. Yet a suggestion that the practices of the industrial world will lead to its destruction is generally regarded as unthinkable, incredible or both.

Another serious cramp in our thinking about the world is our increasingly minuscule perspective on time. Human thinking about time tends to be bracketed by our life span, a hundred years at most. It takes a special effort, for which we need compelling reasons and expert help, to think seriously about anything that happened before we were born or is not likely to happen until after we are dead. And that limited perspective has shrunk considerably in our industrialized, money-based society. Under the influence of a 24-hour news cycle, real-time stock quotes, instant messaging, smart-phone email and Tweets, our time horizons have contracted to those of a fruit fly. Long-term strategic thinking in business extends to the next quarterly statement – 90 days, max. Long-range planning in human affairs gets us to the weekend. Anything that has not happened within the past few years becomes unthinkable as a prospect for the future.

We walk daily, unwittingly, on the bones and among the ruins of people who long before us became arrogant about their ability to bend natural processes to their will. Most of us do so without a thought for the great civilizations – Aztecs, Mayans, Anasazis, for example -- that embraced technology, took control of their world, ate out their resources, and disappeared. Just as evolution in the natural world requires a great deal of dying, so the evolution of human society has involved many crashes. It is, in the long term, normal. Not knowing that is what makes us so confident of our ability to bend natural processes to our will, forever and ever, amen.

Thus far in this book we have examined the frailties of the enterprises that supply us with food, water and energy, and of the institutions that are supposed to help and protect us. We have seen how the once-traditional values and concerns that constrained human activity have been replaced by greed. It is tempting to ignore the evidence of our eyes and ears, to believe that nothing is going wrong, or to refuse to think about it at all. But there is a time when responsible people must confront unpleasant prospects, if they wish to be more than hapless victims of whatever befalls.

A brief fable: You are enjoying a summer stroll across a meadow, alone, on vacation, completely relaxed. A railroad track runs along one side of the meadow. Hearing a train coming at high speed, you glance over and see a small child playing on the tracks. Not your child, not your fault. If you had taken a slightly different path you would not have seen it. Yet your day and your life have been altered forever by a simple piece of information that requires a decision: turn your back, pretend you do not know what you know, and live the rest of your life in torment; or risk your life to try to save a strange child. Rather not choose? Want more time? Sorry, this is the way life comes at us.

So. If it is true that our society is the child playing on the tracks, and the oncoming train is the imminent breakdown of the systems that support its life, then the question becomes when does the train get here? That's a bit like asking the stockbroker who has just explained in detail why the market acted as it did yesterday, what it's going to do tomorrow. It depends.

As we have seen, enormous strains have built up in all these systems. Foreseeing when and where they will actually snap, which one will go first, in which order they will break, is similar to trying to forecast earthquakes. Because of the similarities, and because the crash could actually be brought on by a long-predicted earthquake, let us begin our consideration of when and where the end begins with a look at the natural causes that could be the trigger.

Shake, Rattle and Fall

Long-range forecasting, whether of weather or of earthquakes, is an oxymoron. As with weather, scientists seeking to foretell earthquakes have deployed every available scrap of technology and have pursued with their instruments and formulas every anecdotal clue. Do burrowing animals rush into the open before a quake? Do fish swim erratically, snakes go berserk? Do ponds bubble and wells get cloudy? Does the electromagnetic field warp? Does the region about to be shaken burp radon gas? Sadly, such signs have failed to be reliable, and a prediction of an earthquake at a specific place and time has even less of a chance of being right than a prediction of rain where you are a week hence, which is about 50-50, the same accuracy you would get by flipping a coin. Nevertheless, while meteorology may not be able to guarantee that rain will fall on you today, it can tell you whether you would be well advised to carry an umbrella, or to dive into your cellar for protection from a tornado. Similarly, seismology offers good advice for those who wish to continue living.

A first suggestion would be to stay away from faults – the massive cracks in the earth's crust along which, we have known for centuries, earthquakes happen. If we did that, California would be a national park, visited only by the adventurous, because it is bisected along its north-south length by one of the most active fault systems in the country, if not the world – the San Andreas. As we have understood since the mid-1960s, when the theory of plate tectonics suddenly transformed the earth sciences, faults occur mainly along the borders of 15 huge sections of the earth's crust, called plates, that are constantly in motion. Like glaciers of rock, only much slower, the plates emerge from the planet's molten interior at mid-ocean ridges and rift valleys, and floating on molten rock crawl across the face of the earth until eventually they plunge again into the depths of a subduction zone to melt and start over. It's the ultimate in recycling programs.

At their boundaries the plates are either grinding against each other or ramming into each other. When a plate collides with another it may dive into a subduction zone, or rear up to form a mountain range. In California, the plates are grinding laterally against each other, the Pacific Plate on the seaward side moving north toward Alaska and the North American Plate heading south. As they move, their edges hang up because of friction between their jagged rock edges, bending slowly until the strain reaches intolerable levels and a section of the fault snaps forward to catch up with the rest of the plate, just as a released spring returns to its relaxed state. That's an earthquake. The margins of the plates are not delineated by single, neat faults but by complex webs of fissures and fractures extending laterally over wide areas and vertically for miles into the bedrock. The San Andreas, named and known because it is in many places visible on the surface, is like a mighty river with many tributaries.

The accumulation of strain and its release as earthquakes is a regular process because the velocity of the plates (in California they move past each other at 2.9 inches per year) does not change much. Thus the best indicator yet discovered of when an earthquake will strike in the future is the frequency with which earthquakes have struck in that spot in the past. Along the Southern San Andreas, from Baja California northward to a point roughly midway between Los Angeles and San Francisco, the geologic record shows major earthquakes, about 8 on the Richter Scale, occurring with metronomic regularity (in geologic time, remember) every 150 years. The last one occurred in 1857. Do the math.

(The Richter Scale, that maddening and obtuse method of rating earthquakes, devised by geophysicist Charles Richter in 1935, is a number based on the size of an earthquake's oscillations as recorded on a particular kind of seismograph. It is a logarithmic scale, which means that a magnitude 8 earthquake produces oscillations, and therefor ground movement, ten times larger than does a magnitude 7. On the scale, a magnitude of 2 or lower is barely perceptible, 5 or higher is destructive, and anything at or above 8 is catastrophic.)

In northern California, around San Francisco, the frequency of the big ones along the San Andreas is not known. The last time the city was destroyed by one was 1906, when the fault snapped along 270 miles of its length, displacing its two sides by as much as 16 feet. The tributary Hayward Fault has produced magnitude 7 quakes every 140 years, the last one having occurred in 1868. And the Hayward fault runs directly under San Francisco (the football stadium at the University of California/Berkeley *straddles* the fault, its two halves built separately so they can slide past each other if necessary). In 1906 the lateral movement of the plates snapped the water lines coming into the city, leaving the residents no way to fight the multiple fires, some fed by ruptured gas mains, that consumed it.[63]

Exactly the same thing would happen today: the Hetch Hetchy Aqueduct, carrying water for 2.4 million people, crosses the Hayward Fault.[64] Official estimates of the consequences of a quake the size of the 1906 event include 5,800 people dead, 220,000 homeless, virtually all the bridges and freeways in the area destroyed and the Port of Oakland out of business for a very long time. The Port is the fourth busiest container port in the United States.

A magnitude 7 earthquake near Los Angeles will be much worse. The US Geological Survey estimates that up to 18,000 people would die, every freeway and most railways and gas lines in the city would be destroyed, and damages would total something over $250 billion.[65] That is ten times the death toll, and three times the damages, of Hurricane Katrina, the costliest and one of the deadliest hurricanes ever to strike America. And it would be far worse than Katrina in many more ways:

- There will be no notice, no evacuation, no boarding up of windows or shopping for supplies. Everything will be normal one minute and destroyed the next.
- More than half of the losses incurred in Katrina were insured; in the San Francisco Bay area only about 8% of homes and

---

63 Achenbach, Joel, "The Next Big One," *National Geographic* April 2006
64 Mason, Betsy, "California is Due for a Katrina-Style Disaster," *Wired* 10/20/08
65 Cover Story, "The Day California Cracks," *Business Week* 09/19/05

businesses are insured for earthquake damage.[66]

- According to a USGS study, less than 10% of people living on and near the San Andreas have made a plan for surviving the next big earthquake, and less than half have set aside some provisions such as water, batteries, or first aid kits.

- When Katrina came ashore, it made a choice, and by choosing New Orleans spared, say, Galveston. But the earthquake that strikes Los Angeles will in no way reduce the peril to San Francisco.

Let us be clear: this is not something that might happen, these earthquakes are going to happen. The scientific consensus on this is far older, and more complete, than that on global climate change. Journalists who occasionally do a story on the impending earthquakes do not feel it necessary, in order to appear fair and balanced, to scour the warrens of academe to find someone who denies it all. But there is no corresponding certainty about when it will happen: it is as likely to happen one minute from now as 30 years from now.

The difficulty is illustrated by the closest thing we have had to a laboratory experiment on earthquake predictions and precursors. It took place at Parkfield, California, located at the California midpoint of the San Andreas, a place that likes to call itself the earthquake capital of the world. In the 1980s, scientists realized that Parkfield had a Magnitude 6 earthquake every 22 years, and the last one had been in 1966. Everybody got ready for 1988. They set up cameras and lasers and seismographs and strain meters and radon detectors – every tool in the seismologist's kit was deployed, and then some, to record the quake itself, and any pre-earthquake signals of its imminence, in excruciating detail. The quake occurred right on time, in geologic terms – in 2004. Its epicenter was miles from the predicted spot, and it broke south to north, defying the cameras that had been set up to record it breaking north to south. And it gave no preliminary sign whatever.

---

66 *op. cit., Wired*

All of which enables the people who live along the San Andreas to awake to another day in denial. Asked whether he had made any preparations for the disaster, one worthy told the local paper he didn't need to, because there was a convenience store on his corner.

They are not the only ones. It is not only the water and gas lines going into L.A. or San Francisco that will snap in the Big One; the supply lines for everyone living west of the Mississippi River run in large part through the ports of Los Angeles, Oakland and Long Beach. For the reasons discussed in Chapters One and Five, a substantial interruption of oil and food supplies to a major chunk of the country may not be repairable. The combination of burdens – treating the casualties, housing and feeding the refugees, putting out the fires, repairing the infrastructure -- while the larger economy freezes up ever farther to the east for lack of essential supplies, could bring down the entire shaky edifice of our industrial world.

Not to worry. There's a convenience store on the corner.

The Great State of Denial

There are many other possible triggers for the coming crash. The California earthquake was discussed first here not because it is the most likely but because it is instructive at many levels. It demonstrates that certainty that something will happen does not necessarily translate into knowing when it will happen. It shows how easily people live in denial of substantial risk when there is no large financial interest in making them worry about it. And it illustrates the variety of illogical axioms people embrace in order to avoid confronting reality, including:

- "The longer a thing has not happened, the less likely it is to happen." In fact, with earthquakes and other manifestations of accumulated strain, the longer the thing does not happen the more likely it becomes, and the worse it is likely to be.
- "If I survived a thing once I can survive it again." Popular in

hurricane country, this mantra does not take into account the many differences between one thing and another.

- "Whatever happens, someone will come to save and help me." This was pretty much dispelled in New Orleans after Katrina.
- "If it's that important or dangerous we would be hearing more about it." This confuses freedom of speech with freedom to be heard. In general, with brief exceptions, those who get heard are those who have the money to buy the time and space. They – the people who are developing subdivisions and building power plants along the San Andreas – have no interest in warning you away from their projects. Similarly, processors of food, abusers of animals, wasters of water, guzzlers of oil and the like are not about to buy commercials describing the accumulating dangers of their ways of doing business. So we don't hear much about it. So how bad could it be?

In the book thus far we have detailed the accumulating strains on our various support systems, and have explained that it is not possible to predict the time and place of any final breakdown. Now we are looking at the various ways in which the crash could be triggered, not for the purpose of predicting which one it will be or when it will come, but for the purpose of identifying precursors that should spur us to action. When the tornado watch has been issued, we must watch the western sky for black clouds swirling down. When the warning has been issued, and we see the funnel cloud, it is time to act.

The War on Water

Hurricane Katrina was not the perfect storm She was not the most powerful hurricane in Atlantic Ocean history, she ranked sixth. Not the largest ever, but the largest of her strength. Not the deadliest, but in the top five, and the most murderous since 1928. She did the most damage ever, measured in dollars, but that has more to do with our habit of building things in the path of hurricanes than with the destructiveness of hurricanes.

It could have been much worse. Had Katrina come ashore perhaps 50 miles farther west, and had its course taken it north along the Mississippi River, two things could easily have occurred. First, the storm surge and the most vicious winds, which are found to the right front of the storm's center of counterclockwise circulation, came ashore east of New Orleans. Had they struck the city head-on they probably would have breached the seaward levees, not just the Lake Pontchartrain flood walls, with resulting destruction and loss of life far beyond what actually happened. Secondly, flooding of the Mississippi from heavy rains upriver could have overwhelmed the levee systems of several more cities, with consequences as dire as were experienced by New Orleans. And one more thing.

There is an event coming to the Deep South that is as inevitable, and as imminent in geologic time, and as unpredictable in human time, and as dangerous to human life and enterprise, as are the Great California Earthquakes. It is as easy to say as it is hard to imagine: the Mississippi River is going to change course, and when it does will reach the sea 65 miles west of New Orleans, at Morgan City. This meandering of the the great river is not at all unusual – it happens frequently in geologic time – and is the process that created the Mississippi River Delta – a 200-mile-wide, three-million-acre arc of coastal wetlands stretching roughly from Lafayette, Louisiana, east to Biloxi, Mississippi. As the river nears the Gulf of Mexico, on the flat coastal plain, the current slows, allowing its massive loads of silt to settle out, creating new wetlands and building up the river bed, which eventually becomes higher than the surrounding area. Eventually the river breaks out, seeks a new and quicker way to the Gulf until the process repeats in about a thousand years.

In the 1950s the Mississippi was ready for another change, exploring in ever greater enthusiasm the Atchafalaya River basin. But this time the river had a new enemy: money. If the river succeeded in doing what it had always done, it would leave high and dry the Port of New Orleans, devastate the city's economy as well as that of Baton Rouge, cut off nearly 20 per cent of the country's oil imports and 16 per cent of the nation's fisheries harvest, and choke off a major outlet for US Agricultural exports. It would leave high and dry a chain of refineries and factories stretching from Baton Rouge to New Orleans that depend for their existence on the barges and the fresh water that the river wants to give to the Atchafalaya. It was, well, unthinkable. The Congress ordered the US Army Corps of Engineers to go to war with the Mississippi. "We are fighting Mother Nature," the Corps declared in a promotional film, "It's a battle we have to fight day by day, year by year; the health of our economy depends on victory. Our opponent could cause the United States to lose nearly all her seaborne commerce, to lose her standing as first among trading nations."[67]

The result of this declaration of war was named, with typical Corps hubris, the Old River Control Structures. The Old River was a natural east-west channel that had opened between the Mississippi and Atchafalaya Rivers about 200 miles above New Orleans. By the 1950s, 30 per cent of the Mississippi's flow was roaring down the steeper, lower Atchafalaya drainage, scouring it ever deeper, getting ready to switch its course entirely. The Corps' war on water consisted of throwing a dam across the Old River, then building, 10 miles upstream, a 560-foot-long set of 11 floodgates across an artificial channel that henceforth would bend the Father of Waters to the will of the United States Congress. That body declared it illegal for the Mississippi to yield more than 30 per cent of its flow to the Atchafalaya. That is how much it gave up in 1950, and by law, for the Mississippi, it was to be forever 1950. The implementation of the law began in 1963, when the Control Structures took over. It was all part of the Corps of Engineers' "Mississippi River and Tributaries Project" -- the war to end all floods for all time from Cairo, Illinois, to New Orleans.

---

67 McPhee, John, "Atchafalaya," *The New Yorker* February 23, 1987

Ten quiet years followed, for which the Corps took a great deal of credit. Then came a most unquiet year, when a combination of heavy rains in the fall of 1972, heavy winter snow and repeated deluges in the spring of 1973 brought massive flooding. The Corps ran up the white flag and opened all the floodgates at Old River, and still, day after day, the Father of Waters hammered on the bars of its cell, shook the structure as if it were in a Magnitude 8 earthquake, threw nine-ton boulders at it and ate away at its massive foundations. If you stopped a car on top of the control structure (yes, there's a road – Route 15 – across what you might call the bridge to San Luis Rey, Louisiana) and opened the car door, the shaking would slam it shut. One of the massive walls that gathered the flow of the Mississippi in to the floodgates collapsed. When the whole thing was a whisker away from total failure, the waters began to recede.

Afterward, the badly frightened engineers of the Corps wondered how close it had been. As John McPhee described one of the more riveting moments in the long history of man's war on nature:

> "As soon as the water began to recede they set about learning the dimensions of the damage. The structure was obviously undermined, but how much so, and where? What was solid, what was not? What was directly below the gates and the roadway? With a diamond drill, in a central position, they bored the first of many holes in the structure. When they had penetrated to basal levels, they lowered a television camera into the hole. They saw fish."

The Corps propped the structure up, poured more concrete, set more pilings, built even more floodgates (the so-called auxiliary structure, deployed in 1986) and saw it withstand major flooding in 1983, 1993 and 1997. But the river will win this war, and will go to Morgan City, and bring down the Control Structures and with them the economy of the United States. As a study conducted by the Water Resources Research Institute, at Louisiana

State University, concluded: "It could happen next year, during the next decade, or sometime in the next thirty or forty years. But the final outcome is simply a matter of time and it is only prudent to prepare for it." 68

Blowing the Top

Another event that is past due, in geologic terms, and has the potential to bring down the US economy (again, not by itself but in the manner that an opportunistic infection can dispatch a chronically diseased human) is the eruption of the Yellowstone volcano. Yellowstone National Park lies atop one of the largest volcanic systems in the world. It is an enormous pool of magma – molten rock – just a few miles down, that periodically wells up to the surface in a titanic volcano. Much of the land area of the park is actually a caldera, the bowl-shaped remains of the last eruption of the volcano, which occurred 640 thousand years ago. The rim of the caldera – the shattered remain of the flanks of the mountain that blew up – forms an oval about 50 miles long and 35 miles wide, oriented southwest-to-northeast with Yellowstone Lake along the southern boundary.

Yellowstone has been the site of three of the largest volcanic eruptions to occur in North America in the past two million years. They occur about every 600 thousand years, give or take, and when they blow they bury a significant portion of what is now the United States in ash, and belch enough volcanic gas and dust into the atmosphere to darken and chill the entire planet with devastating effects on agriculture.

Because the interval is so much larger than, for example, that between major earthquakes on the San Andreas, 600-thousand years versus 150, and the margin of error of any prediction correspondingly larger, it is a lot easier to ignore the threat of the Yellowstone "super volcano," as the media have dubbed it. Until, as happened in late 2008, a so-called "swarm" of earthquakes –

---

68 McPhee, John, "Atchafalaya," *The New Yorker* February 23, 1987

about 400 of them – indicate that the magma bubble is inflating and rising. Then there follows a period of nail-biting at the US Geological Survey.69

Catching the Wave

There is considerable disagreement among geologists about the prospects for an Atlantic Ocean tsunami that could devastate the east coast of the United States. The worry is focused on the Canary Island of La Palma. The eruption there in 1949 of the Cumbre Vieja volcano opened a fault that cracked the mountainous 280-square-mile island virtually from end to end. Some studies predict that when the volcano erupts again, as it will, a enormous chunk of La Palma will fall into the ocean, raising a tsunami that will be 35 – 50 feet in height when it reaches the US East Coast. The hypothesis is hotly disputed. 70

Flu in the Coop

Any number of illnesses, diseases, toxins, parasites and critters have the potential to break out into a threat serious enough to start the crash. Thanks to the massive dosing of livestock by industrial agriculture, mutant, virulent, and/or drug-resistant varieties of staphylococcus (MRSA), *E. coli,* salmonella, avian flu, H1N1 virus are already sickening and killing people around the world. One of them, or some mistake made by a genetic "engineer," or some germ we don't even know exists, could come out of nowhere to cause mass casualties and massive contraction of trade.

When the Watched Pot Boils

I have not spent much time here on global climate change (which is one, and only one, of the ill effects of massive, chronic

---

69 *Time Magazine,* "A Spurt of Quake Activity Raises Fears in Yellowstone" *January 1, 2009.*
70 *Geology News,* "Atlantic Ocean Tsunami Threat," *www.geology. com_.*

air pollution) for a number of reasons. For one thing, I am convinced that by the time its full effects are felt, one of the other threats described herein will have got us. Secondly, there is nothing significant that we or any other country on the planet will do to counteract pollution-induced climate change, indeed we have probably reached the point where nothing we could possibly do would mitigate it. The process, intensified by multiple feedback loops, is under way and will run its course. However, its onset is already applying additional strain to vital systems.

The southwestern drought is intensifying water shortages and will soon impact food supplies. Moderating winters have allowed the mountain pine beetle to destroy millions of acres of forest in the West, far northward into Canada. The northward migration of tropical weather is bringing Africanized bees, fire ants and tropical disease such as Dengue Fever to the South. Melting polar ice, which is proceeding faster than the worst-case predictions of just a few years ago, will soon make itself felt at low-lying ports such as New Orleans (which is also sinking, thanks to human mismanagement of the Mississippi, but that's another story). The increased heat energy in the atmosphere, released as more frequent and violent hurricanes, tornadoes, even thunderstorms, will place increasing human and financial stresses especially on Atlantic coastal states.

For some time to come these will probably continue to be small, incremental increases in strain, much like the gradual creep of the tectonic plates that meet at the San Andreas Fault. It is impossible to know when these factors will reach a breaking point, or to imagine the consequences when they do.

Not with a Whimper, but a Bang

The world has never seen a better demonstration of the benefits of terrorism than it did on September 11, 2001, when a country that could not be challenged frontally by any military power on earth was mauled within an inch of its life by 19 guys in four airplanes. The entire country was convulsed by terror. I was told by the proprietor of a tiny country store in the backwoods of the Shenandoah Valley that she couldn't sleep at night for fear of an attack *on her store.* We reorganized our government, we gave up fundamental rights for which our forefathers suffered a hell of a lot more casualties than we did on 9/11, we began for the first time in our history to imprison people without trials and to torture prisoners. In the aftermath of 9/11, our reaction destroyed more of our country than any terrorist ever could, and that could happen again.

Other acts of terrorism and war in the offing pose far graver threats to our survival. In the short term, any effective effort to interrupt or restrict our oil supply – by interdicting the Strait of Hormuz, for example, or ramping up the crisis in the Niger Delta – could bring us down. In the longer term, access to diminishing supplies of oil, water, productive land and food in this country and around the world will increasingly involve significant armed conflict. It is not well known that it already has, with serious and widespread fighting in China, Russia and even India. Every industrialized country (except Costa Rica, an exception that should be better known and more often cited) has an army, and will without hesitation use it to try to restore vital supply lines, whether inside or outside its borders. If history is any guide, the effect will be to destroy the resource they are trying to retain, but they will do it nevertheless.

Keep an Ear to the Ground

Whatever the trigger, wherever the fault slips, the crash will come quickly thereafter. Anyone who wishes to survive it must be ready, willing and able to move quickly into sanctuary. And that means the sanctuary must be ready.

Chapter Ten: Sanctuary

Here is the light at the end of the tunnel: although we can't save the industrialized world, we can save ourselves. The Titanic is going down, but we know how to build a lifeboat for our family and our community. What we need now is the will to undertake the job, the knowledge to do it and the skills to complete it.

The job is to live sustainably, which means living in such a way that we can continue to do so. It requires us to re-enter a relationship with the web of life, first by acknowledging that we cannot take from it more than we give, that we cannot fully understand it, and we cannot ever pretend to run it. It means living in the world, not on it, treating it as a living organism of which we are a part, not as a machine created for our convenience. It means taking into our own hands responsibility for providing our own food, water, shelter clothing and energy without destroying anything. That does not mean that we can't take an animal for our food, but it does mean that we can't wipe out a whole species of animal because it annoys us.

We have to abandon completely the relentless search for economies of scale, which concentrate risk, and head resolutely in the other direction: toward the practicalities of small, the rewards of diversity, the frugalities of proximity. We have to do this for ourselves at first, against a powerful tide, and eventually, perhaps, we can do it with and for our country.

Many primitive societies have lived sustainably for millennia, not out of any noble intention or superior knowledge but mostly because there were not enough of them to do their surroundings any lasting harm. Today we have the knowledge and the tools to live sustainably much more comfortably than they did – although their deprivations have been much exaggerated by the purveyors of cheap energy and instant gratification. The most difficult thing we have to do in order to survive the coming crash is to renounce the life of artificial luxury that has been the temporary product of the systematic destruction of our life-support systems. We have to do it now, because for those of us who are not Amish farmers or Australian Bushmen it will take years to prepare for an event that could begin at any moment. We also have to be prepared to carry the burden of doubt and ridicule that will attend our choices as the countdown to Armageddon, unheard by most, goes on...and perhaps on and on......

Accept No Substitutes

Our hope is in sustainable living. This has nothing to do with "sustainable development," which has become an oxymoron in the hands of industrialists who have co-opted the term to use as greenwash for doing business as usual. For example, as the *New York Times* reported not long ago,[71] subdivision developers have discovered that they can get more cash for a postage-stamp-size lot if it is somewhere near something that can be called an "organic"

---

71 "Organic Farms as Subdivision Amenities." *New York Times* June 30, 2009.

"farm."In one of the featured examples, a developer is preparing to sell 334 homes on 220 acres in Vermont. The farm amenity consists of 16 acres which the newspaper describes as "not previously used for farming," which may mean it was not usable for anything. A 220-home project near Atlanta is going to feed its inhabitants from a 20-acre "farm." The developers are hiring farmers, or perhaps people who play farmers on television, to do something bucolic and organic on these scraps of land within view of the picture windows surrounding them.

The irony here is that the notion of setting aside land for agriculture near our subdivisions, had it been done seriously and from the start, could have brought us all to a far different place. As discussed in Chapter Four (Waste Water, Want Water), The Clean Water Act of 1972 envisioned ending water pollution in the United States by using such fields of growing things to reclaim waste water without discharging pollution of any kind. We could have done it, too, but the developers killed the idea of setting aside any land, anywhere, for any thing other than maximum profits. But now, nearly 40 years later, seeing that we yearn for green, the industries that are trashing the planet give us greenwash.

Similarly, the electricity industry has discovered that the massive new transmission lines they've been wanting to build are vital to getting renewable energy to market. The wind, it seems, only blows in Texas and West Virginia, and the sun shines only in the desert Southwest. So what industry proposes is to build enormous solar plants (using millions of gallons of water) in the desert, enormous wind farms in Texas and West Virginia, and massive transmission lines connecting them with, and extending, the existing and increasingly decrepit grid. Renewable energy may be a part of this equation, but it's a tiny part, and there is nothing renewable or sustainable about this set of plans.

The Will
The will power needed to begin the quest for sanctuary -- a

place in which sustainable living is possible -- is considerable. We have to leave the ship, and it's not an easy choice. The decks are still above water, the band is still playing, there's more steak and champagne to be had at the buffet tables, and people are having a good time rearranging the chairs. But we have to go. By which I mean, decide. For a time we will still be in the world, sampling the last of its delights, but because we know the ship is going down, we must begin our preparations. Remember my little fable about the walk in the meadow, during which you spot a child on the tracks in the path of a speeding train? There is no time in that scenario to have a debate with yourself about the ethics and the ramifications and the permutations of the situation. It will not do to say to yourself, "Well, after I enjoy a few more minutes of my walk I'll do something." Once you know, you must act. It takes time to build and equip a lifeboat. We have to start yesterday, and proceed at warp speed.

The last time the American people were required to change their way of living in order to survive was during World War II. The great majority of our predecessors accepted privation, rationing, high taxation, involuntary limits to and changes of their occupations, even injury and death, in order to resist tyranny and sustain their way of life. They were led in this effort by a charismatic president, and sustained in it by a government that used all available channels of communication to inform and encourage them. There were leaders and prophets and patriots among them, urging them on and constantly defining the cause that was greater than them, more valuable than money, and worth their sacrifice. They prevailed.

The stakes today are easily as high -- nothing less than survival. The effort required to prevail, however, is much greater because our leaders are heading relentlessly in the other direction, our institutions will do anything they can to resist the changes that can save us. Chronic infectious greed, expressed in unrestrained industrialism, has emaciated the programs and processes designed to protect the non-rich, while it has been decimating the web of life upon with the rich and non-rich alike depend for their survival. What we must do we must do alone, or in small groups, without the support of our money-crazed society.

Many people will remain age-optimistic, telling themselves that if they're lucky, they'll be dead before the crash happens. Most will cling as long as possible to blissful ignorance, drinking champagne and watching the movie until the screen goes dark. Are they really the optimists here and we, who see what is coming and are ready to make our preparations, the pessimists?

No, for two reasons. Because we understand that evolution can only work though the death of the ill-equipped, we can see what is coming as a transition to a healthier, more fulfilling life lived in concert with the world and not as its mortal enemy, lived free of the haunting knowledge that the way we are living cannot go on. Secondly, if enough of us embrace the necessity to live sustainably, and if the gods of chance grant enough time before the inevitable collapse of industry, it is possible – not likely but possible – that our efforts could produce in the society at large a paradigm shift toward a viable way of living. There is always hope, there are always reasons to be optimistic, but hope and optimism are empty declarations unless they are grounded firmly in necessary work.

There's the Will. Where's the Way?

If you are going to create a sanctuary, you are going to have to learn a great many things you have not needed to know before. And the knowing is not limited to the acquiring of information. You can read all the gardening books there are, and it will not prepare you for the myriad faces of crop failure. (Lewis's First Law of Agriculture: If you do everything right you might get a crop; if you do anything wrong you will not get a crop.) To learn gardening – and sanctuary requires that you grow your own food -- you have to do gardening for years, so start now. For many this is unfamiliar territory, but it is easily explored and mastered. Gardening, animal husbandry, preserving and storing, butchering, hunting: these are the skills in which you need doctorates now. You will be gardening without chemicals, irrigation systems or roto-tillers; cropping without fertilizer, plows or even tractors, and raising animals without force-feeding them alien foods, putting them in concentration camps or drenching them with medications.

You are going to have to be able to use tools to build and repair your shelter and your machinery. You are going to have to learn to manage electricity and repair plumbing and understand weather. In the words of Robert A. Heinlein:

> "A human being should be able to change a diaper, plan an invasion, butcher a hog, conn a ship, design a building, write a sonnet, balance accounts, build a wall, set a bone, comfort the dying, take orders, give orders, cooperate, act alone, solve equations, analyze a new problem, pitch manure, program a computer, cook a tasty meal, fight efficiently, die gallantly. Specialization is for insects."

Whenever the need for sanctuary presents itself, tomorrow or ten years from now, you will wish you knew more. So start learning right now, and go hard.

While you're learning, change the way you think about money. Accept the fact that after the crash it won't matter how much money you have because it won't be worth anything. To prepare for that day you need to spend money, and you must avoid making decisions, as so many people do, based on lowest price, enhanced status and instant gratification. For example, forget such calculations as return on investment, or time to recoup the investment, when you are pricing sources of energy, food and shelter: the return on this investment is called survival. Priceless.

(Why is it, by the way, that considerations today of buying solar panels or hybrid vehicles always seems to involve a lengthy analysis of how long it will take to recoup the investment? The calculation never seems to come up when one is buying a Hummer or a hot tub.) The things we acquire in order to provide sanctuary must stand on their own and they must last, and that implies that they will be simple things, mostly tools, of high quality. Think in terms of shovels, and forget flat-screen TVs.

Cleared for Land

When you have decided to go for sanctuary, and have started the learning, you must decide where. Let's consider where *not* to go.

Sanctuary is not to be found in any city or suburb, dependent as they are on massive quantities of cheap energy, food and water, all brought from afar. You are going to need to buy or rent a piece of rural ground, and before you do, think long and hard about its location and nature. Sanctuary is not to be found on the Atlantic or Gulf coasts or barrier islands, because the water is rising and the hurricanes are going to be more frequent and powerful; nor on the Pacific coast because the water's rising and because it's on the edge of a tectonic plate and thus subject to frequent earthquake and volcanic activity. Sanctuary is not to be found downstream from any sizable dam, if its collapse will submerge your property, or behind any stretch of levees (pretty much without exception, levees were shoddily built to minimal specifications and have not been maintained), or indeed on any floodplain.

Sanctuary is going to be hard to find in the Southwest, where increased consumption of depleted water supplies already threatens the continued existence of cities and agriculture, and will do so increasingly whether or not the region becomes drier and hotter as forecast. Sanctuary is going to be problematic in previously ideal settings along the western mountains because of the shrinkage and possible disappearance of the snow pack that replenishes the area's rivers and streams.

If you have decided to move to your sanctuary and live there as you develop it, you have plenty of territory left from which to choose, and we'll discuss the further evaluation. But if your decision is to straddle the bet by remaining for the present at your city job, and preparing a sanctuary somewhere nearby on weekends and vacations, please think again. You would be asking the gods to give you an extension of time that may not be within their power, even if you spend all the weekends and all the vacation time working on your sanctuary as you might now intend but will not do. Moreover, unless you are so well informed and hyper-vigilant that you know when the collapse has begun 24 hours before anyone else, you are going to have a very hard time getting to your sanctuary when you need it. Once the balloon has gone up, and everyone understands what is happening, no one will be able to move on a major highway in a congested area. If this is the way you have to do it, you must find a place within a relatively short drive, and be as ready as the average rabbit to dive into your hole if you think the time has come. The burden of doubt and ridicule attending false alarms will simply have to be borne.

The first tangible step toward sanctuary is acquiring a piece of ground. Now you're not dating anymore, you're talking ring on the finger -- a serious and visible commitment. You're not going to have time for a long courtship, so you'll need a really good background check. A first consideration has to be privacy. The more the better. You do not want to be anywhere near a major road, not within miles of an Interstate Highway, and the fewer strangers who can see your place or what you are doing there, the better. This is probably the place to point out the obvious -- that there is a security component to sanctuary -- and to add that I am not going to have anything to say about that. It is not an area in which I have any special knowledge. You will make security arrangements according to how you view your fellow humans and the situation you find yourself in, and I see no useful way to generalize about the possibilities.

As well as private, it has to be good ground, much or most of it fertile, level and well drained. If you expect to heat with wood, it has to have an area of hardwoods sufficient to yield a sustainable harvest of firewood. If you plan to have grazing or browsing animals, there must be some open pasture that is, or can be, fenced. There must be a good sized garden plot of really good ground. Think through your food requirements and specifically how you are going to meet them, and then make sure your ground can provide it. There must be enough arable land to feed its occupants – five acres is probably the smallest desirable acreage, although one could do with less.

There must be fresh water. Surface water -- a stream, pond, lake, river -- is highly desirable, because it offers the possibility of energy generation and additional food, such as fish,. But you must be aware of where the water comes from, and what possibilities exist for its pollution or diversion. I know someone who found out too late that the babbling brook that crossed his new property emerged from an abandoned mine up in the mountains, and was highly toxic to all living things.

If you must rely on well water, fine, but make sure it's available ands drinkable before you buy. Better to risk a few hundred dollars finding and tasting the water than to rely on the assurances of the seller that everybody always finds water. They don't, and some who do either don't want to drink it (high sulfur content does not make the water unsafe, but it makes some people gag), or cannot (because of contamination). You must provide a way to get the water to your house and your animals without outside energy sources: a hand pump will work fine for a shallow well, or you might need a solar-powered pump for a deep one.

You are also going to have to decide, based upon the location and the nature of your property, how you are going to provide your energy needs without recourse to the grid. If there is a windy ridge on it, you're going to want to deploy a wind turbine; if a vigorous stream, a water turbine. Just about anywhere is suitable for solar panels for electricity and solar collectors for heat -- just make sure your building site is not perched on a north-facing ridge, but has plenty of exposure to the southern sky

If your property meets all these requirements and in addition offers a nice, spacious rambler -- too bad. You would be better off bulldozing it. Industrial housing is almost impossible to retrofit for sustainable living. To begin with, industrial builders pay no attention to the siting of the house, and orientation to the sun is essential to efficiency. The typical house is too big, is an energy guzzler, and altogether a nightmare of inefficiency. You will be much better off buying raw land and building. However, if you like the land, and the cost is not prohibitive, you could live in the house that's there while you build the one you need.

Let's assume you've completed the analysis and have bought or otherwise nailed down the land for your sanctuary. You have your water supply, an eventual food budget, and an eventual energy budget. The next priority is shelter. I'm going to presume you're building from scratch, because I hope you are.

A Home is Not a (Standard) House

One of the requirements of sustainable living, and of separation from the industrial world, is to realize that one size never fits all, and only one size fits you. Like all other industrial products, the modern house is designed primarily for the convenience and the profit of the builder. And this has been true for so long we seldom even think about the important stuff:

- One wall of the house should have lots of windows, and the opposite wall should have almost none. The window wall should face due south, the other side (are you still with me?), north. This applies, of course, to the Northern Hemisphere, and primarily to the temperate and northern latitudes. The reason is to get maximum solar gain through

232

the south-facing windows in winter while reducing heat loss to northerly winter winds.

- Beyond the bare necessities -- a bedroom must have room to lie down, a kitchen needs a sink, etc. -- the size and number of the rooms must be no more than your energy budget permits. This applies to the height of the rooms as well -- you will be heating and cooling the entire space. Do not despair at this, you'll find that it is possible to be comfortable in much smaller spaces than we have become accustomed to; and once you're used to thinking about your energy sources as you do your food supply (How much do I have? Do I really need to use this? etc.) it will become second nature.

- There are lots better ways to build a house than with 2 x 4 sticks. Logs, straw, rammed earth, block, brick, adobe -- check what's available where you are and what is appropriate for your climate. Super insulation is a primary consideration, and dirt does that as well as anything. Personally, I think a single story structure, bermed to the north and west, with two feet of earth on the roof, would be close to ideal.

So you understand now -- sanctuary is not to be found in a faux-Victorian mansion of five thousand climate-controlled square feet with multiple bathrooms, a great room and sauna. Think a thousand square feet, super-insulated, bermed if possible, facing the sun for passive solar gain when needed, heated by wood or with solar collectors. The new sustainable houses that don't need heating, that are becoming popular in Europe, are a possibility, but they require a sophisticated heat exchanger that would be a big part of your energy budget, and that would disable the house if your electricity supply failed (the humidity would increase and the air would grow stale).

There is another, vital consideration for planning a

sanctuary. Community.

In the colonial period of this or any other country, it was very rare for one family to go alone into unknown territory, strangers in a strange land, to begin a new way of living. They went in wagon trains, to form settlements and communities and towns, and we must learn from their experience, and that of most of human history during which people have organized themselves in clans. To prosper and be safe, we must re-create real community. Whether this consists of family, family and friends, or some other population, we must be numerous enough in our sanctuary to divide our labor, to have the ability to care for the elderly and the sick, to populate a baseball game or a barn dance.

School for Hard Knocks

It is beyond the scope of this book to take you through all the steps of creating your sanctuary (that may be the next book). But if I have succeeded in getting you to look down the road toward a safe haven, and to consider the choices necessary to get there, then let me offer you some road maps for the terrain between you and there.

Get to know about Joel Salatin. Log on to his website *www.polyfacefarms.com* and learn about what he's doing and why. Buy and memorize his book, *You Can Farm*. Understand how, by letting animals be what they naturally are and do what they naturally do, he gets unbelievable productivity from ground *whose fertility he is simultaneously improving*. Visit and take a tour of his farm if you can, there simply is no better example of sustainable agriculture.

Buy a copy of *Back to Basics* (Readers' Digest Association, 1981). I have a grubby yellowed copy of the first edition, and a spiffier copy of the second edition (2003), and there are not many things I undertake on my farm that do not involve a preliminary check with *Back to Basics*. Evaluating and buying land, utilizing renewable energy, raising animals and plants for food, food preservation and storage, it's all there and a lot more.

Read Barbara Kingsolver's book *Animal, Vegetable Miracle*. She and her family decided to live for one year exclusively on food they produced themselves. They did it, and so can you and I, especially with the excellent (and funny) advice of a great writer who did it first.

Form community with the people in your area who practice sustainable agriculture, who use renewable energy, who garden organically, who fuel their cars with vegetable oil, who practice water harvesting. Meet them and learn from them and join hands with them. It's going to be a wild ride, and we will all need someone with us when it's over.

So Here We Are Then

We got to this place that cannot be sustained by accepting and responding to and rewarding a set of assumptions that seemed self-evident and beyond challenge, in a world that has embraced them for ten thousand years. Among the most important of these dicta, to cite them in the order they probably became current during those millennia:

- *The world is a machine* whose workings, although complex and beyond our reach given the current state of our technology, are comprehensible. And as soon as we know something about how part of the machine works, we can take that part of it over because a cause always leads to the same effect. Which is to say that there is no such thing as unintended consequences.

- *To succeed, specialize.* It makes no sense to know a little bit about a lot of stuff. To get the big bucks, raise a single crop or a specific animal, to the exclusion of everything else. Then when you need to know about something from another field, like why all your corn is dying at once, you get the advice of the best experts, and spend big bucks buying whatever chemical or machine they're selling, and do whatever they tell you to do. Experts will never lead you astray.

- *Go for the economy of scale.* If you make a lot of things, each will cost less than if you made just a few things. Farming a thousand acres may put you so far in debt you'll never get out, but you'll be spending less per acre than if you were farming a hundred acres. Whatever the cost, whatever the obstacles, at every opportunity expand, and pretty soon you'll be too big to fail.
- *The only measure of worth is the dollar.*

To doubt these principles, so firmly established in our culture, seems heretical. To deny them, as I have done here, will, to some, seem criminal. God help the politician who raises questions about them, she would be driven from office and then into exile as an un-American apostate. Yet observe the outcomes of these golden rules: vanishing soil, dead and dying waters, deteriorating quality and rising toxicity of food, total dependence on vanishing resources (oil, water, etc.), crushing debt and the increasingly real and present danger of famine.

The achievement of different outcomes requires the adoption of different guiding principles:

- *The world is an organism* whose relationships, in their number, complexity, variability and subtlety, are orders of magnitude beyond our ability fully to comprehend. We need to study the world not to achieve mastery of it, but to live in it without upsetting the exquisite balances of the systems that nourish us.
- *To succeed, generalize.* Never tunnel your way to knowledge, stroll toward it with your peripheral vision fully engaged, asking always how what is seen relates to what is unseen, how what is here relates to what is there, remembering always the importance of the unknown.
- *Strive for sustainability.* Nature does not support economies

of scale. Rather than exerting themselves to get bigger, natural systems tend toward balance, with every organism limited to an appropriate size and number.

- *Measure nothing with money.*

I can think of no better benediction as we part company and go toward what awaits us than the words of Abraham Lincoln in his Second Inaugural:

"The dogmas of the quiet past
are inadequate to the stormy present.
The occasion is piled high with difficulty,
and we must rise with the occasion.
As our situation is new, we must think anew, and act anew.
We must disenthrall ourselves
and then we shall save our country."

www.ingramcontent.com/pod-product-compliance
Lightning Source LLC
Chambersburg PA
CBHW070953040426
42443CB00007B/486